# CHRISTIANS
# AND JEWS

# CHRISTIANS AND JEWS

## *The Eternal Bond*

Stuart E. Rosenberg

Foreword by Rev. Theodore M. Hesburgh, C.S.C.

Frederick Ungar Publishing Co. / New York

For my mother,
KATE ROSENBERG

and in memory of my father,
HYMAN ROSENBERG

The first edition was published under the title
*Bridge to Brotherhood:*
*Judaism's Dialogue with Christianity*

**Library of Congress Cataloging in Publication Data**

Rosenberg, Stuart E.
  Christians and Jews.

  Rev. ed. of: Bridge to brotherhood. 1961.
  Includes index.
  1. Judaism—Relations—Christianity.
2. Christianity and other religions—Judaism.
I. Rosenberg, Stuart E. Bridge to brotherhood.
II. Title.
BM535.R63   1985        296.3'872        84-25278
ISBN 0-8044-5800-6

# Foreword

This extended essay on mutual understanding is clearly the result of years of personal bridging on the part of its author, Stuart Rosenberg, the articulate leader of a cosmopolitan Toronto synagogue. A synagogue, or *shul,* is a place for learning, above all, the word of God, so that its leader, the *rabbi,* must regard himself as a teacher. And that we find in Dr. Rosenberg, yet more. For we find an even-handed expositor, who can write for Christians as well as for Jews, illuminating the faith of each to the other.

It is that skill which cannot be learned in graduate schools, though their training may provide a baseline for gaining experience later. What Rabbi Rosenberg displays can only come through a loving exchange with believers of another faith. And as readers will discover, when they are enlightened about their own situation on nearly every page, few are the individuals who have the courage to bridge the cultural and theological chasms that have over the centuries eroded contact between Judaism and Christianity. A visiting professor at Notre Dame in the late 1970s, himself the descendant of several generations of Jerusalem rabbis, had to confess that this was the first time he had spent any time at all in a Christian environment. And we for our part had to acknowledge that only one out of our extensive number of Christian theologians had studied Judaism in an explicitly Jewish milieu. We had invited the professor to visit in order to strengthen our doctoral program in Judaism and Christianity in Antiquity, yet none of us had quite realized the nature or extent of the gaps to be bridged.

There are reasons for the prevailing state of affairs, to be sure, and Dr. Rosenberg sketches them deftly in his historical background notes to ''sacred places.'' Few Christians, for example, will realize that Judaism in fact postdates Christianity, so that at least some of the postures we associate with synagogue, while rooted in the Hebrew Scriptures, were in fact developed in reaction to the sect of Jewish believers in Jesus. Rosenberg delineates this intertwining skillfully, alluding as well to the way in which criticism of current Jewish institutions has become enshrined in the New Testament.

It is here that I believe Dr. Rosenberg's study can profit us most, by its focus on moments sacred to human becoming and on sacred times and seasons. This is the world that Catholics and other Christians honor with sacraments, and it is itself noted in the form of blessing peculiar to Judaism: the *beraka*. Following the pattern of Moses interceding with God on behalf of God's own people—by reminding God of what God had already done for them—the sacramental practice of Christians is a living commemoration. Hence it is rooted in the Passover celebration, which formed the living context for Jesus' giving himself to us in the eucharist. Yet the fundamental rhythm of prayer that shapes the lives of every Christian turns on a weekly celebration of that saving event. And that pattern of weekly celebration of the life-giving activity of God was already enshrined in the sabbath observance. If Christians chose the first day of the week—the day of Jesus' resurrection—rather than the last, they nonetheless adhered to the Israelite pattern of one day out of seven. Moreover, the manner of celebrating that day has been various among Christians, but a semblance of the "day of rest" has perdured. This is crucial to note, not only in the face of commercial erosion of that sense of repose, but to remind Christian readers how the New Testament polemic against the sabbath, put invariably into the mouth of Jesus, regarded features of that practice quite specific to the time of Jesus and of the early Christian community. As a practice—a reminder to us all that the world we seek to improve does not itself come from our hands—the repose of the sabbath is relinquished in Christian or in Jewish communities only at their own considerable risk.

As one impressed enough with the Holy Land to have

spent countless hours and untold effort to establish there an Ecumenical Institute for the Study of Theology and, even more recently, a Center for World Peace, I continue to be fascinated by the power of that land—the place where Jesus walked the earth—to align one's theological speculations with the realities of history. Oscar Cullmann, the originator of a school of biblical theology called *Heilsgeschichte* ("history of salvation"), came to see how this approach could easily be swallowed up in abstractions without a complementary *Heilsgeographie* ("geography of salvation"). And it is Judaism that must continue to remind Christians of the irreplaceable character of sacred places, since our penchant for celebrating God's universal salvific will readily lead us to global horizons. That tension between the particularity of a Jesus who was not, remember, himself a Christian, but a Jew, and the universal scope of His Gospel, must continue to nourish Christian theology. For without it, the sacred can easily be construed to emerge from the merely human aspirations for something more.

Finally, Dr. Rosenberg's book bridges what will remain genuine differences. And to his credit, he makes no attempt to minimize those—another result of continuing and authentic dialogue. Yet in spite of the differences in belief, the fact remains that Jews and Christians share a trajectory of salvation. Articulated in the cryptic phrase of the statement of Vatican II on other religions (*Nostra Aetate,* par. 4), that "God does not repent of the gifts He makes or of the calls He issues," and enshrined in the unbroken practice of Christian prayer, which has never found a substitute for the Psalms, the God who saves is the God of Abraham, Isaac, and Jacob—and Jesus; and that same God cares for us all.

However, in the time since this book first appeared Christians have come to a far more acute appreciation of the tenacity of prejudice in our midst, and of the roots of the abominations of Auschwitz in those mindless evasions of responsibility on the part of Christians. Jews, for their part, have gained considerable foothold in global politics and history, becoming in the process acutely aware of their own injunctions to care for "the stranger in their midst." As each community examines its conscience with regard to the other, let them both be alert to the madness that has overtaken a world without faith, in its penchant to rely on violence and on a multiplication of weapons, in the putative search for peaceful coexistence. May Christians and Jews, by their fruitful exchange with one another and their candid recognition of differences, offer a witness to other ways of resolving difference, and even join hands to extend that witness to others.

*(Rev.) Theodore M. Hesburgh, C.S.C.*
*President, University of Notre Dame*

# Contents

# Introduction

Many people perform the sacred rites and customs of their ancestral faith without an awareness of the way in which these practices developed in the historical past. They are often unaware of the manner in which their own rituals are related to those of their neighbors around them, whose patterns of religious behavior seem to be different, sometimes even strange.

Most Christians, it seems to me, have a hazy notion that Jesus was a Jew—but beyond this, they have not the slightest idea that, after all, Christianity not only emerged out of Judaism, but inherited its basic tradition and viewpoint from the mother religion. In many and varied ways, the developing Christian church moved away from its origins, leaving its Hebraic past far behind. But what seems to elude many people is the fact that, without a proper understanding of their own Jewish sources, Christians can hardly expect to know very much about Christianity.

I find, of course, that many Jews are equally ignorant of the way in which Christianity is related to their own faith. As a result of this lack of knowledge, they tend to view Christians from a distance—a distance which creates a chasm of total apartness. No man need be quite like his neighbor; indeed, he cannot be. But neighbors who are, indeed, brothers and sisters might at least be helped to understand that fact.

While our culture and society have been fairly well secularized by modern democracy, Christianity is still the dominating religion. As a result, the impression is often given that non-Christian groups are really "minority religions," and are not to be taken too seriously or thought about too carefully. Wisdom teaches, however, that no one can really know what he stands for, unless he sees himself in relation to others. Thus, an understanding of our many-sided *relationships*—our need to make comparative evaluations and mutual adjustments—is of the very essence of the democratic ideal. Because being in the majority can delude us into believing that we can go it alone, Christians, in particular, have the need to adjust to the fact that other religions also exist.

But of all the other religions in America, it is about Judaism which Christians need to know the most—and this for at least two reasons. They surely require an understanding of the kind of spiritual life their Jewish neighbors practice, for the proper understanding and appreciation of differences is of the very essence of democratic life. But even more important is the fact that, given an understanding of the Jewish sources of Christianity, Christians can gain a clearer perspective of their own religion and come to appreciate their own rituals in a deeper and more mature way by seeing Judaism not as a rival but as a partner.

Jews, too, require a keener knowledge of their own tradition in order to perpetuate their ancestral faith in the midst of a world dominated by other denominations and churches. An exposition of Judaism for the benefit of Jews, which takes into account its impact upon the religious life of the non-Jewish world in which they live, is more vivid and instructive than a mere recitation of facts or procedures; what is more, such an approach helps point up the significant truth that a living Judaism continues to exert an influence on the world today as it has in the past—no Synagogue, no Church!

Theology and philosophy, however, are not the metier of the average churchgoer, and a discussion which is based only upon arguments for truth often throws more heat than light upon the subject. In addition, it is too often Olympian, vague, and abstract. Like most people, churchgoers need to "see" or "hear" ideas before they can begin to understand them. We learn best by moving from an examination of form to an understanding of content; often the form itself easily suggests the content. The reverse condition, however, is not always true: Christians may vaguely remember that Jesus lived and died as a Jew; but how does one live and die as a Jew? When the Christian comes to grips with this question, he can begin not only to understand the Jew, but truly to understand Christianity.

In offering this approach to the religious life of Jews, I pray that it may serve as a guide to a clearer understanding of Judaism for both Christians and Jews—that they may learn to cherish the eternal bond that links each to the other, and both together, to the one God of all.

*PART 1* SACRED PLACES

# 1 Temple and Synagogue

The first area to be examined in attempting to learn more about the way in which Judaism functions is caught up in the simple question: what is the synagogue and how did it come into being?

Modern Jews sometimes refer to their synagogues as temples. This is not quite accurate, for it was only in Jerusalem that the Jews had a Temple. It was the pivotal religious center of the people, and it was unthinkable that any other institution could surpass or replace it. It was there, atop Mount Zion, that the priests, descendants of Aaron, and their assistants, the Levites, received the sacrificial offerings of the people. Each day, morning and afternoon, sacrifices took place upon its altar under the supervision of the priests. But the Temple precincts were particularly thronged at the time of religious pilgrimages, when families from all over *Islam* the land converged upon Jerusalem. These pilgrimages were related to the harvest calendar, since the Jews, at that time, were primarily an agricultural people. They came to the Temple in Jerusalem at the beginning of spring, at the time of the first harvest in early summer, and again at late harvest time in the fall, to seek God's blessing for a season of bounty.

Until the fall of Jerusalem in 586 B.C.E., this Temple which Solomon had built stood for over four hundred years. Within two generations, under Persian rule, a second Temple was erected on the same site as the old one. This new Temple, enlarged and made even more magnificent by Herod (20 B.C.E.), stood until the Romans conquered Jerusalem some ninety years later.

There was an air of splendor about the Temple. The priests and their vestments, the Levitical choir and orchestra, the *magrepha* (organ?) whose tones overflowed the chambers, the incense, the libation, and the golden altar added to the majesty surrounding the service. Toward the conclusion of the service, the priests, bearing the vessels used at the altar, raised their hands as high as their shoulders and recited the priestly benediction. It was then that the High

Priest, beautifully attired and wearing a breastplate adorned with precious stones, offered the libation of wine. As he commenced this ceremony, another priest unfurled a kerchief-like flag and cymbals clashed. The Levites sang and the orchestra played. Then there was a pause—a trumpet sounded a sharp blast and the people in the courts prostrated themselves. At each pause there followed a trumpet blast, and at the notes of the trumpet the people fell to their knees, prostrating themselves. They had come from afar to Mount Zion, often at great effort and expense; but to be able to come so close to the Holy of Holies, to feel the presence of the indwelling God, to join in happy fellowship with their people from all over the land, was adequate reward for the pilgrims.

There was only one Holy of Holies, only one place where sacrifices to God could be made, and this was in the Temple at Jerusalem. Those who had been exiled to Babylonia after the fall of Solomon's Temple, and possibly even some who lived in Palestine—but at a distance from the Temple—naturally had difficult access to it. But they could draw near to God in other ways. They could, for example, gather in their homes on the sacred seventh day of the week, the Sabbath, to read to each other from the Scrolls of the Law and the writings of the Prophets. After reading from these texts, the head of the family might interpret some portion of the sacred text by means of homily and exegesis.

Out of such humble beginnings, a new institution to be known as the synagogue arose. In contrast to the Temple it was exceedingly simple, for it was a "portable sanctuary" which did not require a fixed place, nor were specific physical forms or shapes ordained for it. At first, it was not identified with a special building, since it came into being wherever a congregation consisting of ten family-heads joined together for study and for prayer. Elaborate and detailed descriptions of the plan of the sanctuary that was to be the Temple and rigid rules governing its officiants, the priests and Levites, are to be found in the Hebrew Bible. But the synagogue grew without forethought, plan, or design, without an established hereditary or hierarchical clergy. Nor was it a protesting, rebellious institution, claiming for itself the role that had been assigned to the Temple. On the contrary, its prayer services were modeled after the Temple service and were said twice daily—morning and afternoon—at the times of the sacrificial offerings. (Later, a third service, recited after sunset, was added.) As a result of the destruction of Herod's Temple, the synagogue liturgy came to include the recitation of daily prayers for the restoration of the ancient and Biblically-ordained institution, for only in the Temple could sacrifice be offered to the Lord. The orientation of the meetingplace was toward Jerusalem as a continuing reminder of the supreme sanctity of the Temple, but while the furnishings of the synagogue might be similar to those of the Temple (as a link in the chain of tradition), they could not actually imitate them. There was no altar in the synagogue because there could be no sacrifices; there might be a candelabrum, a *menorah*, but it could consist only of five, six or eight branches, and not seven, like that of the Temple.

It was fortunate for the survival of Judaism, however, that the synagogue had succeeded in becoming an accepted public institution before the Temple was finally destroyed. It had attained an independent position as the seat of worship of quite a different character—a place of rational worship and study which did not rely upon sacrifice. As an organic part of the service, regular instruction in the ritual and moral laws of Scripture had been introduced; and, in fact, this practice came to be its most prominent feature and distinguishing characteristic. The development of such a center of worship had immeasurable consequences for the subsequent history of civilization. For the Jews, it meant that the fateful day when the Temple walls were razed by Titus did not augur the end of their unique religious way of life; the synagogue was there to breathe new life and new hope upon them. For those who later were to be known as Christians, the synagogue directly and indirectly determined the type of worship which they were to establish. As we shall soon see, the first Christians worshipped at the side of their fellow Jews within the synagogue and thus, from its very beginnings, the synagogue was to be an important influence upon Christianity. More than half a millennium later, the synagogue, in part directly, and in part through the church, furnished the model to Moslems when Judaism's second daughter religion was prepared to set forth as a distinct entity.

From the very outset, the synagogue, as distinguished from the Temple, was governed by laymen, not by priests. At the helm of each congregation there was generally a council of wise and respected men known as "elders," or *presbyteroi,* in Greek. Their numbers varied from place to place but they were never fewer than three, including the chief elder who was known as the *Rosh Ha-Kenesset,* or the "archisynagogus." The latter was called upon to maintain order, assign seats, distribute the various honors, and invite teachers and preachers to address the congregation from time to time. He was obviously not a clergyman in the professional sense, nor was he required to be a religious teacher, or rabbi. He was subject to the control of the entire congregation to which he had to render an account of his activities and his management of its finances.

A second functionary, attached to most congregations, was the assistant to this chief elder, a kind of factotum who was principally charged with providing elementary instruction to the children. In addition, it was his task to rouse the faithful to services, publicly announcing the times by means of a trumpet blast. In the synagogue's earliest days this official, known as *hazzan,* or cantor, sometimes chanted the liturgy before the congregation. It was this last activity that, in a later era, came to be identified with the office of cantor. Since the average worshipper, in those days, still knew how to recite the weekly Scriptural reading when he was called to the Scroll of the *Torah* (Pentateuch), the *hazzan* had only to carry the Scroll to the one called upon to read, and then to indicate the proper place. This procedure is no longer practiced in the modern synagogue, which now employs a professional Torah Reader.

The synagogue arose in the midst of a democratic religious community, where universal literacy supplied the key for popular and widespread participation in the conduct of the public worship of the Jewish people. This explains why it is not possible to talk about the rise of the synagogue without discussing the second of the great institutions of post-Biblical Judaism—the school, which, in some form or other, is surely as old as the synagogue; and the synagogue, clearly, was dependent upon it.

The very nature of the synagogue service demanded an educational support beneath it, a reservoir from which could be drawn the living waters of the Tradition. Philo of Alexandria and Flavius Josephus attest that when the Second Temple stood, universal instruction for young boys was already an established practice. While organized schools may not have emerged until the second pre-Christian century, there is evidence that regular academic gatherings were held earlier in private houses, not only in Palestine, but also in the Babylonian dispersion. "Get thyself a teacher and take unto thyself a fellow student," was a popular Jewish adage of the day.

When schools did develop, they were placed adjacent to the synagogue; virtually every synagogue had a school of its own. And in keeping with the religious ideals of the rabbis, it was the school which was superior—thus, a building occupied by a synagogue could be transformed into a school, but the contrary was not true. It was considered a descent to a lower degree of sanctity to convert a schoolhouse into a synagogue.

It was customary for a community to provide an elementary school teacher for the first twenty-five boys over six years of age, adding an assistant teacher for forty children, and still another instructor if the number should exceed fifty. Often, as indicated earlier, it was the *hazzan* who served as the elementary school teacher, as well as the synagogue attendant.

The curriculum of these schools was arranged by the rabbis. In accordance with a long established custom, children were first introduced to the reading of the Hebrew Bible by beginning with the Book of Leviticus. From the Five Books of Moses, the instruction progressed to the books of the Prophets and the Hagiographa. The elementary school was indeed a Bible school.

Even greater attention was given to adult education. To attend the *Beth Ha-Midrash* (House of Study) or academy of higher learning, was the aspiration of most of the people. Here, scholars exchanged views with one another, disciples put questions of the Law to their masters and were also given the opportunity to express their own opinions. The master continued to regard himself as a student, and if he found brilliant disciples he was ready to sit at their feet. The *Beth Ha-Midrash* contributed to the recognition of the meaning of equality for members of the community, and learning became more than sophistry—it served as an instrumentality for the spread of democratic, humanistic ideals. "Take heed of the children of the poor, for from them will come forth the word of God," was a favorite epigram of the academies. Thus the object of learning was not merely scholarly erudition, but the refinement of character. These Pharisee-teachers were not, as some maligners suggest, self-righteous, arrogant men. Modesty, simplicity, even austerity were considered by them to be the most becoming attributes of the student. They taught: "This is the path of the Torah: A morsel of bread with salt shalt thou eat; thou shalt drink water by measure, and shalt sleep upon the ground; and live a life of trouble while thou toilest in the Torah."

General literacy, thus, led to democratic participation in

synagogue life. The school and the synagogue combined to serve as joint centers of learning and worship. But they were more. They were to be continuing sources of spiritual and ethical wisdom.

## ii How the Church Emerged from Judaism

Such were the synagogues and their officials at the time of Jesus of Nazareth. His religion was the religion of Judaism, and he undoubtedly received his instruction and religious training in a synagogue very much like these. This was a time of great speculation over the coming of a Messiah, and the first followers of Jesus were Jews who earnestly believed that he was the Messiah foretold in their Scripture. There were other religious-minded men whom other Jews considered to be the divinely-heralded messenger in this time of evil, when the power of Rome cast its spell throughout the world. But the followers of the others did not attempt to establish a new religion apart from their own Jewish community as did those who adored Jesus. How this came about has an important bearing upon many things which we shall be discussing later. It is also important in understanding how it was that the Church emerged out of the Temple and the synagogue.

The Jewish followers of Jesus were known as Nazarenes. At the outset, they comprised a small group in a Jewish community already divided into a number of different sects. Jesus himself undoubtedly followed the general principles of one of the larger groups, the Pharisees, or separatists. Because he was deeply influenced by them, even in a little Galilean town like Nazareth, he was able to become learned in the Law and to know his Scripture. The Pharisees, for the most part members of the lower classes, were intent upon making the Torah the inheritance of the whole house of Israel and not merely the private possession of a small group. This is one reason why they chafed under the power wielded by the Sadducees, the aristocratic, priestly party, named for Solomon's high priest Zadok. These Sadducees were totally identified with the Temple, its worship and its organization. The Pharisees, on the other hand, respected the place of the Temple in the spiritual realm, but denied that only members of the priestly group, the Sadducees, had the authority to act as judges of the people and interpreters of the divine law.

In their academies, devoted to the study of Scriptural Law, the Pharisees slowly established themselves as the religious teachers and judges of the people. Just as the synagogue came to fill the religious void created by the fall of the Temple, so the views of the Pharisees, who emphasized that the study and application of the Law was of equal importance with the Temple service, came to replace those of the Sadducees in the days following the destruction of Jerusalem. The Pharisees, the accepted teachers or rabbis of the community, replaced the priests, the Sadducees, as its leaders, and the literature they created is known as the Talmud. In the Talmud, their viewpoint is expounded over and over again: The Temple might fall but God would not forsake his people as long as they did not forsake His Law—the Torah; Rome might destroy the state and wipe out its national life, but Judaism would not be overwhelmed, for the synagogue and the academy could take the Torah into exile and survive any physical onslaught.

But there were some Jews who splintered off into smaller cell groups, and did not abide by all of the doctrines of the new teachers—the rabbis. Some, like the Essenes, practiced a primitive communism and emphasized extreme ritual purity and non-contact with those less observant and uninitiated in the ways of the group. A still smaller number, like the followers of John (who came to be known as the Baptist), emphasized a mystical, apocalyptic idea: The power of evil had reached its zenith, the land was about to be destroyed by Rome, and nothing less than the ushering in of a new kingdom—God's kingdom on earth—by mysterious and miraculous means, would accomplish the ultimate goal desired. John, and others like him, despaired of any other solution to the problems the Jewish community faced; repentance was the first need of the hour, for the kingdom of God was near at hand.

In the earlier Jewish messianic tradition, the Messiah was conceived as being a mortal man, chosen by God to lead his people as a model king of the house of David. He was to be the prince of peace; and peace would come when God's Law, the Torah, became the Law of all men and all nations. He was to elevate the Jewish community to such a spiritual height that it might become a light unto the nations, the leader in establishing and maintaining a warless world. To herald the coming of this Messiah, the prophet Elijah would return to earth. It was Jesus whom John identified as the anointed one, the new Messiah-King. And John's followers thought of him as Elijah who had come to proclaim the age of peace by announcing that the Messiah had come.

On the eve of his death, which was possibly also the Jewish Passover, Jesus joined with his leading disciples, twelve in number—symbolical of the twelve tribes of Israel—in a meal of fellowship. At this, his last supper, he gave them important instructions. Following the style of Jewish homily, which is fraught with the symbolical suggestiveness of material objects, he referred to the bread and wine on the table, ascribing to them a significance which now endowed them with mysterious and supernatural meanings—meanings Jews had never before understood them to have.

> And as they were eating, he took bread, and blessed and broke it, and gave it to them, and said, "Take; this is my body." And he took a cup, and when he had given thanks he gave it to them, and they all drank of it. And he said to them, "This is my blood of the covenant, which is poured out for many . . ."
> (Mark 14:22–24, R. S. V.)

Soon thereafter, Jesus was arrested by Roman soldiers, and his companions fled in fright and worry. For both Romans and Jews, this was a most strained time—the streets of Jerusalem were flowing with pilgrims for the festival of Passover, and Jewish discontent with Rome had never been more pronounced. Pontius Pilate, the local governor, was hardly an easy man to deal with. In fact, he was to be removed from his position by Caesar himself, some time after, because of his accumulated record of unnecessary cruelty. Jesus was viewed by the Roman governor with great suspicion, since a popular Messiah, or would-be King of the Jews, was not only an affront to the Caesar, but a dangerous and subversive force who could easily ignite a wild fire among his people, which might lead to open rebellion.

It is important to note here, as many modern Christian and Jewish scholars do, that the accounts of the death of Jesus, as recorded in various places in the New Testament, cannot be read without recognizing that these were not eyewitness reports, but were written years later in an atmosphere filled with acrimony. For in the years which intervened between the death of Jesus and the earliest of the gospels, Mark, relations between the early Christians and the Jewish people became very strained. It has been suggested by scholars that this came about for at least two reasons: on the one hand, Jews officially refused to accept Jesus as the Messiah, while on the other, because it was hoped that Christianity might become an acceptable religion in the eyes of the Romans, attempts were being made to read the events surrounding Jesus' death in a way which would absolve Rome of serious guilt.

Indeed, the "great Christian-Jewish tragedy," as one Christian scholar puts it, the tragedy which was to mar the relations of these two religions over long and difficult centuries, was perhaps unavoidable at the time, owing to the historical circumstances. The death of Jesus is a blatant example of Roman oppression of the Jews—for Jesus was executed, not as a Christian, but as a Jew! Ironically, it was this very oppression which later generations of Jesus' followers sought to justify by exonerating the Romans of the death of their Messiah. In the process, however, the blame for his crucifixion was put upon the Jews—his very own people.

But objective scholarship, interested in setting the ancient record straight, and not motivated by the desire to fan the fires of hate which were kindled by this ironical tragedy of

[13]

history, has now proved that the Jews did not crucify Jesus. The crucifixion was committed by Pontius Pilate, and the trial of Jesus by the Sanhedrin (Jewish Court), as described in the New Testament, cannot be squared with other known facts of the period: Trials of Jews would scarcely have been permitted to take place on the eve of a festival, the Passover; and, as we shall see later, a death sentence by the Sanhedrin was virtually a rarity, and in view of the so-called charges against Jesus, an impossibility. That there were individual Jews who did not agree with Jesus and who even disliked or feared him, we may accept. After all, there were many sects and religious opinions among them at this time, and religious diversity has always characterized the Jewish people. Yet scholarship testifies to the massive facts which point to an inescapable conclusion: it was the Romans, not the official Jewish community, who saw in Jesus a treacherous Jew who threatened their political rule; it was they who took him prisoner, found him guilty and put him to death on the cross—the Roman method of capital punishment.

After Jesus was crucified by the Romans, the older Jewish idea of a victorious Messiah was transformed by his disciples into a new concept—"the suffering Messiah." At first, his followers placed their emphasis upon his death and upon his miraculous resurrection on the third day, confidently looking forward to his quick return—he died on Friday, and his friends and disciples believed that on Sunday, the third day, he had risen from the dead, and would return again soon.

Like many other Jewish sects of the time, his followers maintained their own separate identity; yet for many years after his death they continued to remain loyal to the Jewish community. They recited the same prayers all pious Jews did, and came to worship in the Temple as did their fellow Jews; they attended synagogues, kept the Sabbath, and observed the Jewish festivals. How then, did the break come—a break which was to result in the founding of a new religion with its own distinctive theology?

This was to come about with the growth of a new institution—one which at first saw the founding of the Church as a separate fellowship within the synagogue, and later as a religious community apart. At the close of each Sabbath, those Jews who believed that the Messiah had indeed come, and that his name was Jesus, withdrew to their homes to join in a love-feast, known in Greek as the *agape*. It is customary, in Judaism, to offer thanks at the beginning of festive meals by praising God over bread and wine, symbols of the bounty of field and vineyard. But the followers of Jesus infused into this Jewish ceremony a specific messianic significance by recalling the new mystical meaning which Jesus had applied to the bread and wine during his last supper. By means of this mystical ritual of memorial, the followers of Jesus became intimately tied to each other by the bonds of a new religious fellowship. Because it stemmed from the original Jewish practice of thanking God for the gift of food before partaking of a meal, this ritual took the name *Eucharist*, which, in Greek, means "the giving of thanks." This additional ceremony, performed only by those who were known as Jewish Christians, came to be celebrated each week as a regular memorial to Jesus. It took place on the first day of the week, Sunday, to recall the "third day," the day Jesus rose from the dead. Thus it was that Sunday came to be known by Christians as the "Lord's Day."

Years later, sometime before the end of the first century, these home rituals were transferred to a public service which was conducted by the followers of Jesus every Sunday morning. What was to be the basic content of these services? We shall soon see how their services were based largely upon the Jewish practices most early Christians had known before they left their ancestral community, and were modeled, in part, after the Temple service as well as those rituals which were current in the synagogue. Those who sought to identify

[15]

themselves with this new religion by joining the church were also required to undergo an initiation patterned along lines which were also derived from Jewish practice. The new Christians were "catechized"—given a systematic course of instruction followed by immersion in water, the symbol of the beginning of a new life. Thus baptized, the new Christian considered himself part of the new Israel which, for Christians, became synonymous with the real Israel. From this time forward, the paramount concern of the developing church became its mission to "make disciples of all nations." All references in earlier Jewish writings to the mission of Israel were now considered to apply to the church—the new Israel.

In the Greek and Roman world, Jews had engaged in numerous missionizing activities. Many outstanding Roman nobles, as well as members of royal houses, had adopted Judaism as their own religion. Among the rabbis themselves, there was a goodly number of converts or children of converts to Judaism. Indeed, Jews never forgot that Ruth, the ancestress of their great King David, born a Moabite, had been a member of a nation which had perennially fought Israel before she voluntarily accepted the God of Israel and the people of Israel as her very own. Ruth's classic proclamation of loyalty still remains a favorite quotation from the Hebrew Bible: "Entreat me not to leave thee and to return from following after thee; for wither thou goest I will go; and where thou lodgest I will lodge; thy people shall be my people, and thy God my God; where thou diest will I die, and there will I be buried . . ."

Instruction in the law and customs of the community was an integral part of the Jewish conversion rite, and for male converts circumcision was also a preliminary religious requirement. After these obligations had been fulfilled, final conversion to Judaism was consummated by means of a ritual of immersion, or baptism. At the conclusion of baptism, after all the other requirements had been met, the new convert to Judaism was considered to be a full-fledged member of the community, as if he had been born a Jew. The rabbis of the Talmud ruled that "he who has been immersed emerges as an Israelite in every respect."

Yet, in spite of this "open-door policy," there was never complete unanimity among the ancient rabbis with regard to active missionizing programs. There was always the fear that if Judaism officially adopted a policy which urged vigorous missionizing among non-Jews, the religious ideals of Judaism might be compromised for the sake of gaining new members. The Jewish religious mission, in the eyes of the rabbis of that time, was not geared to conversionary activities; it was rather their desire that Judaism be made an influence upon the non-Jewish world so that all men might become more receptive to its universal teachings. They were extremely cautious and conservative, for they believed that they would have to dilute these truths if they were to engage in special efforts to win over the pagans. They feared that, rather than turning from idolatry, the pagans might retain some of their heathen practices in coming over to Judaism, and thus destroy the higher and more subtle meanings which monotheism taught.

The persecution of the Jews instituted by the Emperor Hadrian represents a turning point in the history of active Jewish proselytizing. In 132 c.e., the Roman Emperor promulgated bans against public Jewish religious instruction, as well as against circumcision. These edicts made it most difficult for Jews to carry on their own religious life; they were now placed on the defensive. It was difficult enough for those who had been born Jews to continue their own religious practice; now it became even more difficult to seek to make new converts to Judaism.

Christianity, on the other hand, from its earliest beginnings was concerned with the need to "Christianize" the world. Paul considered that the very essence of the new religion was its universal saving qualities, believing that the world stood in need of redemption and *all* peoples could come to God only through *"the* way"—through faith in Jesus. At the very core of Christianity there stood the cross, the sign of salvation, which was to be carried to all—pagan and Jew alike. Until the time of Hadrian, throughout the Roman Empire Judaism and Christianity had been rivals in gaining new adherents. After the decrees of the Emperor had been promulgated, Jewish missionizing activities continued, but at a much slower pace, until they almost disappeared as a perceptible force in the Jewish religion. On the other hand, the Christians pursued prospective proselytes with unremitting zeal and vigor. Moreover, since conversion to Christianity had never required circumcision, Hadrian's anti-Jewish decrees did not hamper the spread of the Christian mission; on the contrary, it indirectly helped to pave the way for the expansion of Christianity which was to follow in the time of Constantine.

What was the structure of the churches into which these large numbers of converts were now coming? Obviously, as in so many other areas, the government of the church was patterned along the lines of Judaism. But which form of Judaism—that of the Temple or that of the synagogue? The earliest Christian congregations were governed along lines paralleling those of the synagogue which, in contrast to the theocratic structure of the Temple, was established along more democratic lines. A board of elders, popularly elected, comprised the earliest leadership group in the church— very similar to the arrangement in the synagogue. The leader of the synagogue, the *archisynagogus,* was delegated by the other elders to act as the head of the congregation—in modern parlance, he would be called "President." In the church, the head of the congregation was known as *episkopos,* or bishop, the Christian counterpart to the *archisynagogus.* A member of the board of elders of the Christian congregation was called *presbyteros.* Thus, at first, the bishop or *episkopos* was the equivalent of a president popularly elected by his fellow ruling elders. But when the tasks of governing the congregation became too numerous, as a result of the increase in the number of converts, the elders required additional help. Deacons were added to the leadership of the congregation to help the elders carry out the many new functions.

By the end of the first century, however, the more loosely organized Christian congregations began to formalize their earlier patterns and, in the process, they departed from the pattern of synagogue polity, and reverted to the earlier Jewish model—the government of the Temple. The bishops, elders and deacons now came to form a threefold ministry, and they alone were authorized to conduct the Christian ritual. The church now followed the political organization of the Temple where priests and Levites comprised the ecclesiastical elite, and where they alone were authorized to lead the congregation in prayer.

Within a few years, by the middle of the second century, the Church moved even more closely toward a hierarchical structure. Bishops, who at first lacked a strong, centralized position, now came to enjoy a large increase in power and authority. This development seems to have come to pass as a result of historic necessity. Owing to the growing heresies within the Church, the bishops were required to take a firmer stand against these defections from the tradition. As a consequence, the greatest men of the time were drawn into service as bishops, and they, in turn, helped to defend the faith against the incursions of the heretics. Their stalwart defense increased the authority of the bishops' office and added stature to their special position. The theory of apostolic succession was now asserted: the bishop is the heir of the spiritual gifts of the early Church and, through the succession of bishops, the continuance and preservation of the authority of the first Apostles is assured. By now, the bishops had succeeded not only to the seats which the Apostles filled, but also to the power they possessed.

The synagogue, on the other hand, continued to move further away from the earlier Jewish form of religious polity, and placed responsibility for the management of the congregation in the hands of the laymen. In ancient and medieval times, the synagogue became much more than a center of prayer and a seat of learning. Before long, all of Jewish public life was to take a cue from and find its stage in the synagogue itself. The democratic impulse which it supplied radiated in many directions, and slowly filtered into the philanthropic, political and social spheres of Jewish corporate life.

The synagogue not only preached the virtues of charity, but it also developed a whole network of philanthropic institutions. Strangers and sojourners, wayfarers and travelers were housed in its public shelter, a practice which has continued up to the present day. Committees were formed from its councils to look after a wide gamut of communal philanthropic needs: dowering brides from economically-depressed homes; giving free loans to promising but underprivileged colleagues; providing for burial rites and funeral arrangements for families in dire financial straits; and the supremely urgent and regular requirement of providing funds for the ransom of Jewish captives. A tradition had developed during the first centuries of the Christian Era whereby, every Friday, the poor of the town were given enough food to provide for the fourteen meals of the coming week, and if clothing was needed, it too was given. According to accepted custom, no one who himself had two meals in his own house could be exempted from making a personal contribution to the needy.

Prior to modern times, before Jews were given rights of citizenship, each of their communities was governed as an autonomous tiny republic. The councils of these groups met on the premises of the synagogue and the principles of democratic action were pursued under Biblical sanction. Members could assemble at any time to debate all matters of social concern. Community elections, resolutions of self-government, and discussions of general policies all took place within the walls of the synagogue; courts of law, too, were administered there by the rabbi-judges. Indeed, any aggrieved member of the community, if unable to obtain redress through the court, was permitted to demand a hearing, and was even allowed to invoke the assistance of the congregation by interrupting divine worship if this seemed necessary to insure his right to be heard. If a member was unable to secure necessary evidence for legal purposes, he too, was permitted to rise in the midst of the congregation and seek the help of those who he believed were capable of giving the relevant information.

The synagogue also came to serve as the social center of the Jewish community. Important family events were celebrated there: the circumcision ceremony, initiating the newly-born boy into the Covenant of Abraham, as well as engagements, marriages and the family festivities connected therewith. Even the public baths, used for general as well as ritual purposes, were most often built in or near the synagogue courtyard. For Jews, the synagogue was not something set apart from life, but rather a "second home," an institution whose embrace touched virtually every vital aspect of human life.

Perhaps because the synagogue became so total a reflection of the entire community rather than serving only as its ecclesiastical center, the rabbi never simulated the role of the Temple Priest (Kohen). In any case, he had never been considered as the liturgical leader of the congregation, for he never "officiated" at services. And yet the transition from Temple to synagogue was easily made without a breach in the continuity of Jewish life. For while the rabbi never took the place of the priest, his general religious functions were to become so comprehensive, and thus so influential, that he was bound to be regarded as the Jewish "spiritual leader." Thus, despite the loss of the Temple and the ultimate disappearance of an active Jewish priesthood, no serious disruption took place in the continuity of the religious life of the Jewish community.

We are now ready to turn to an examination of the role of the rabbi and the ways in which it differs from the functions of Christian priests and ministers.

# III The Rabbi

Christians better understand their own religious practices and traditions when they explore the history of the parent from whom it emerged. Thus if one were to seek information regarding the development of the Christian church, he would have to find it within the history of the Jewish Temple and the synagogue. For the church is the product of its own Hebraic past; it came to life, shaped and molded by the cultural and religious heredity of its immediate ancestors.

When one attends a synagogue service, he will be quick to notice that the rabbi of the congregation seems to have little to do with the conduct of the liturgy. This is a most surprising fact to those who are accustomed to ritual services which are led only by the spiritual leaders of their congregations.

Thus, in order for a Christian to understand his own church services more clearly, he should know something of the manner in which the rabbinate has developed and the ways in which the rabbi functions.

Today, synagogues and rabbis are institutionally united—rabbis function within synagogues. In the earlier period, however, at the beginning of the Christian Era, the development of the rabbinate and the synagogue paralleled each other but they had not as yet converged. The priests who had ministered in the Temple had also been the interpreters of Jewish law, not as expounders but as judges. With the destruction of the Temple and the consequent waning of the priesthood, leadership fell into the hands of those who could act as judges. A history must be assumed for the growing class of scribes who began to emerge as an institution set in opposition to the priests. The scribe, by reason of his knowledge of the Law and his technical ability as a student of religious jurisprudence, came to assume the importance once held by the priest. Politically, too, the scribe enjoyed the support of the strong Pharisaic party.

The Pharisees were united on religious grounds, and differed on many points with the Sadducees. However, economic and political factors were even more important than ritualistic or legalistic differences in causing a division between these two sects. The Pharisees were a people's party; the Sadducees represented the last remains of priestly vested interests. It becomes clear why the scribes, who had no priestly connections, were helped to leadership by the Pharisee party.

With the reorganization of the schools after the destruction of the Temple of Jerusalem, in 70 C.E., the scribe was now called rabbi, a Hebrew title for what we might call the "diplomaed doctor of the Law." The growth of this educated class as the accepted religious authority became more pronounced as its leaders, the rabbis, began to exercise juridical rights as well as to expound the Law. When the teacher also became the judge, the high rank of the priesthood was virtually eclipsed. For, in this Jewish society, it was the judge who exercised the widest power and who enjoyed top status.

The Pharisee-scholars did not deprive the priests of the special prerogatives which the Torah gave them as *experts in the laws of purity and sacrifice*. Yet these lay teachers began to fashion Jewish life in such a way that priests and Levites were no longer really indispensable to a living Judaism. The synagogue continued to accord the priests special honor but only in a peripheral way, for it could now continue to function without priests just as Judaism could survive without the Temple. It was now that the schools and academies became the focal point of the community, and in some ways the academies were even more significant than the synagogue itself. Perhaps this is why the Pharisees taught the primacy of the school: they could make more insistent and successful claims to leadership in the religious as well as the secular fields by acquiring the authority to mold both the sacred and the profane aspects of Jewish community life—an authority which the schools were now capable of granting them. The destruction of the Temple was thus only the "last straw"—it helped to bring about the disappearance of a professional priesthood upon which the community had previously depended—a priesthood whose religious authority had been undergoing attack and challenge for some time.

While the school-men, or rabbis, were not yet the spiritual leaders of specific congregations or synagogues as in our day, they were, in many ways, infinitely more important—they served as leaders of the total community. From the schools and academies they forged and shaped the moral and cultural content of Jewish life, far beyond the ritual program of the synagogue—all of which is contained in the Talmudic laws they legislated. In this way, lay scholars, or rabbis, consolidated their position as the authoritative expounders of the Torah, becoming the preeminent judges and teachers, and thus, the leaders of the community.

In our day, most individual congregations are led by their own rabbi who serves as spiritual leader. Yet in the synagogue, as contrasted with the ancient Temple where only priests and Levites officiated, any adult male Jew may lead in the ritual. Indeed, if you attend a weekday synagogue service, morning or evening, you will find that it is usually conducted entirely by the lay members of the congregation. Even on the Sabbath, the most significant service of the week, the rabbi participates in the Hebrew prayers in the same manner as any other lay member of the congregation. There is a fixed ritual to the service, a traditional prayer system which has come down through the ages since the time of the earliest synagogues. These prayers, collected in the form of a *Siddur,* or the accepted order of prayers, are read by every member of the congregation who responds to the leader of the ritual who chants these selections. Most of the prayers consist of excerpts from the Book of Psalms, together with other Scriptural passages. It was customary in ancient Semitic communities to read Scripture by means of a traditional chant. Thus the one who leads the service, the chanter or, as he has come to be known, " the cantor," is generally selected on the basis of his ability to interpret these chants vocally. While any adult male is permitted to lead the musical chant of the liturgy, most congregations engage a professional cantor who serves, in a sense, as a minister of music.

In Conservative and Reform congregations where English (or another national tongue) has been added to the worship, the rabbi occasionally leads in responsive readings which have been interpolated in traditional Hebrew texts. Yet, in contrast to the minister and the priest, the rabbi still appears to be less active in the conduct of public worship. Even the Scriptural lesson, which is read from the handwritten Scroll of the Law containing the Five Books of Moses, is not read publicly by the rabbi, but rather by the synagogue reader. The reader chants the weekly portions of the Law in accordance with a traditional mode or cantillation, whose musical origins go back two thousand years.

What, then, are the ritual and religious functions of the rabbi? It is the rabbi, of course, who preaches the sermon, on those occasions when sermons are given, on the Sabbaths and holidays. And this is the key to his function. "Rabbi" is the Hebrew word for teacher. His preaching is essentially teaching, for his function is to interpret the laws, traditions, and concepts of Judaism in order to help give meaning to all of life in all of its manifestations. Nor is his teaching task restricted to the pulpit alone. In every department of synagogue activity his major function continues, for it is his task to help infuse into the life of his congregation an understanding of Jewish law and tradition. As it is the purpose of the Jewish religion to sanctify life by fulfilling the *mitzvot,* or commandments, so it is the rabbi's function to lead the members of his congregation to a deeper knowledge of the meaning of the commandments, in order that they may perform them in joy and devotion. To be sure, there are groups of rabbis who differ in their interpretation of these laws and traditions. In America, and other Western countries, they are divided into three rabbinical bodies and congregations known as Orthodox, Conservative, and Reform. This division is not so much over matters of creed, since Judaism has relatively few, and in the view of some, only one theological dogma—the belief in ethical monotheism. Their differences, however, are related principally to the manner in which they interpret the Law and the commandments. The Reform interpretation is most lenient, unperturbed by the necessity to break with the past in its earnest effort to "modernize" and "westernize" Judaism. The Orthodox attitude is most stringent, maintaining the eternal relevance of the Biblical and Talmudic teachings for all times and places. The Conservative viewpoint tries to adopt a middle road, desiring to affirm the basic body of these teachings, while attempting to relate them to the conditions of modern life; its aim is to re-interpret the Law wherever possible, in order to make it apply to the current human situation.

Volumes have been and will continue to be written analyzing the philosophies of these three religious groupings in modern Judaism. One can only delineate briefly some of their more salient views. The Reform movement began in the middle of the nineteenth century, chiefly in Germany and America, as a radical answer to the new discoveries in science, history, and comparative religion. It broke with tradition in its attitude to Jewish law in general, and denied the binding authority of the Bible and the Talmud on questions of ceremonial and ritual law. Reformers replaced Hebrew (the basic language of prayer) with the vernacular, as a symbol of their common bond with fellow citizens of other faiths. Dietary laws and other rituals which smacked of social segregation or seemed too oriental for the western mind were omitted from the religious regimen. Supernatural authority was denied as the basis for the ceremonial law contained in the Bible and in the later codes. Reform Judaism has, however, stressed the prophetic values of Scripture and accentuated the historic mission of Israel to serve as the priest-people of humanity.

While the nineteenth-century reformers created a renaissance in Jewish scholarship in their effort to find support for their modern views, some dissatisfaction arose with what was felt to be their one-sided emphasis on Judaism's universalistic teachings, and their seeming neglect of the unique Hebraic character of its spirit. As a result, there grew up in a number of European countries, and more especially in North America, a school of thought which spoke of the need to emphasize the "positive-historical" elements of the tradition. This prepared the way for the growth of what has come to be known as the Conservative movement in Judaism. In contrast to Reform, the Conservatives emphasize the distinctive elements in Judaism, asserting the need to *preserve* the Jewish people as a separate group consecrated by divine commandments, through the unique ceremonies and rituals of the tradition. While they are not fundamentalists in their Biblical views, and are not committed to a literal interpretation of Revelation, they do acknowledge the authority of the Bible and the Talmud.

Because the Conservatives do consider the tradition as a living and relevant way of life, they are often, in practice, not too far removed from the third grouping known as Orthodox. The principal distinction of the Orthodox sector is its strict adherence to a belief in the literalness of Revelation, and its steadfast denial of the role of historical evolution in the field of religion. Yet it must be understood that, even within Jewish Orthodoxy, there is room for differing modes of Biblical interpretation, and even a willingness to search the Law for meanings which may have been lost but which still can help man to live more spiritually. It should be noted that all three names—Reform, Conservative, and Orthodox —are borrowed from the world of Christian denominations and have gained popular currency only in the last century.

The Orthodox, Conservative and Reform groups maintain their own individual seminaries for the training of rabbis and sponsor congregational unions. But since each congregation can elect its own rabbi without regard to any other authority the synagogue is completely autonomous. It is controlled principally by its membership and trustees, and is not subject to presbyterian or episcopal jurisdiction. While the rabbi of each congregation is its religious teacher and interpreter, his authority is principally one of moral influence, rather than of special grace. He is ordained as a rabbi by the faculty of his seminary, to teach and to interpret the Law and the commandments. While each of the three rabbinical groups maintains committees to coordinate its own viewpoint with regard to the interpretation of Jewish law, each rabbi and each congregation is morally free to interpret in the light of their own understanding of the tradition.

No Jewish congregation, then, may rightfully be challenged regarding its authority to speak in the name of the tradition. This is so because the synagogue, unlike the church, does not consider itself as the authoritative or divine instrument for dispensing salvation. If it were, then the following questions would have to be answered: Who authorized the formation of the first synagogue? Can each synagogue verify that it is operating in the name of and by the authority of its first founder? Can the congregation prove that the synagogue is privileged to offer its people the grace of God, because it is itself a divine institution? These are questions which are significant within Christendom. Yet, none of these issues is relevant in Judaism.

To be sure, the Jewish tradition claims the "chosenness of Israel." But it never thinks of the synagogue as the means whereby the chosenness is either conferred or assured. In Judaism, chosenness implies the responsibility which Jews have as a community or group, inside or outside of the synagogue, to bear witness in their personal lives and in their communal association to the oneness of God and His law. And the Jewish tradition insists that this can come about, not through the ordinances of an ecclesiastical unit such as a synagogue, but only by the *personal* fulfillment of the *mitzvot* on the part of the individual Jew as a member of the Jewish community.

Thus the rabbi is not a priest, because he performs no ritual *for* his group—only *with* it. But neither is the rabbi a minister, because he does not act as God's authorized agent in offering access to personal salvation. This is why we have called him a layman. And this is why, both in theory and in fact, ritually his role at Jewish services is of no greater religious consequence than that of the humblest member of his congregation.

The rabbi is ordained by his teachers, but ordained by them to be as one of them—a teacher. This history of rabbinical ordination goes back to the period before the beginnings of Christianity, when it was the custom of each master of the Law to authorize his own pupils to teach publicly by laying his hands upon them. Through this ceremony he granted them what would be the modern equivalent of a diploma, a transference of pedagogical authority from master to pupil. The Apostles of Jesus borrowed this ceremony from the rabbis, and, in accordance with the spirit of Christianity, gave it a different meaning. Laying on of the hands, for the Christian church, came to signify a remembrance of the rite the Apostles used when they wanted to indicate the men whom they had selected as their successors. Since the Apostles received their rights from Jesus himself, and since only they were so selected, it became an issue of paramount importance whether those who were not so selected might administer the divine sacraments of the Church. Indeed, one of the principal difficulties between Roman Catholics and Protestants revolves about the question of "apostolic succession." The Roman Catholic Church challenges the right of those not ordained within what it calls the Apostolic Church to administer the sacraments, on the grounds that they have not been authoritatively ordained to do so.

This whole problem, which is a very serious one for Christians, is totally irrelevant to Judaism. For the rabbi, being essentially a teacher, derives his authority from his own teachers to interpret the Law in the light of the Tradition, as he himself understands it. Therefore, he need not justify his authority by claiming to be in a line of succession which flows from Moses or from any other great teacher of the past. Moreover, since in Judaism, the rabbi does not administer or dispense sacraments or sacred rituals, he is obviously but one of the members of his congregation rather than a representative of the Divinity. Indeed, this is the crucial line of demarcation between rabbis, priests, and ministers. And this difference, in turn, is a reflection of the manner in which Jews differ from Christians in their general interpretation of the functions of organized religion, and the ways in which ecclesiastical authority operates.

The rabbi is not a representative of God to the people; he is a representative of the people before God. Nor does he represent them by any proxy, elective or appointive. He is "a teaching elder" whose role it is to clarify and interpret the Mosaic Law and rabbinic codes to his people. Groups of rabbis may, from time to time, issue rulings on the Law, which virtually comprise new legislation in the form of reinterpretation. But since there is no central hierarchy in the rabbinate, individual Jews are free to accept or to reject such interpretations. The authority of the rabbinate in the free societies is primarily an "authority of influence," rather than an "authority of coercion." This situation, to be sure, sometimes leads to relatively chaotic religious conditions; overindulgent autonomy stretched to an extreme, can and often does result in anarchy. For this reason, from time to time, there have been suggestions that the rabbinate re-establish for modern times the counterpart of the ancient Sanhedrin, which, during the days of the Temple, served as a central legislative body of 71 prominent rabbis who officially codified the Law. On the other hand, there are other Jews, equally loyal to their own religion, who find such an idea abhorrent, claiming that the general freedom of Jews to follow rabbinical judgments in the Law should be maintained, so that democratic competition of ideas can be preserved even in the area of religious life. Consensus, these people urge, is a more valuable goal of free men than authoritarian coercion.

In practice, in North America at least, three wings of modern Judaism—Orthodoxy, Conservatism, and Reform—have evolved as a practical answer to those who sought to find religious self-expression in a congregational atmosphere which would be more congenial to their interpretation of the Law. Thus, while the Orthodox Jew properly disagrees with his Conservative or Reform co-religionists on religious issues which arise from their interpretation of the Law and commandments, he must regard them as dissenters rather than as heretics, as members of the same religious community, rather than as separatists.

Since each congregation elects its own rabbi and is autonomous in its affairs, responsible only to its own membership, no hierarchy has ever developed in the rabbinate. Rabbis assume importance or prominence, not because of any official rank which they attain, but rather as a result of their own personal achievement in the fields of scholarship and moral influence. In certain countries, where there is an established Christian Church, the office of "Chief Rabbi" has developed in response to the demands made upon the Jewish religious community from the specific environment in which they live. In those countries where the clergy of the established religion function as governmental or quasi-governmental officials, it became necessary or convenient for the Jewish community, together with the temporal authorities, to designate a single rabbi who would act as the chief religious spokesman for the Jews in all matters which had a bearing upon the relationship of the Jews to church or government.

Thus, for example, in England and parts of the Commonwealth, in Scandinavian countries, and in lands dominated by Roman Catholics, the office of Chief Rabbi has emerged. In North America, however, where the conditions of freer religious enterprise prevail, no such arrangement has been required. In the State of Israel, where the rabbi functions as an official of the government (since Judaism, in Israel, is virtually the established religion), the office of Chief Rabbi does exist, but primarily for administrative purposes. However, it should be clearly understood that the Chief Rabbi of Israel in no way controls or supervises the religious life of Jews outside of that State.

The ancient Temple fostered a priestly hierarchy; the synagogue substituted learning and piety as prerequisites for congregational leadership. Thus it is that no hierarchy prevails in modern Judaism. At the outset, Protestantism was the heir of the synagogue, rather than of the Temple tradition. Protestants took the view that they were restoring the organization of Christian life to the original conditions which prevailed in the primitive church. In so doing, they were actually following the arrangement which prevailed in the synagogue rather than in the ancient Temple, which was governed by the priestly hierarchy. When Protestants dissented from Roman Catholicism during the early years of the Reformation, they were motivated, knowingly or unknowingly, by the type of religious government which prevailed in the synagogue. To be sure, there are still some Protestant denominations where bishops rule and yet laymen are still assigned many religious duties. This obtains in such countries as England, Sweden, and Finland, where the bishops of the Church accepted the Reformation and thus went over to the Protestant side, retaining their place as bishops. But in other countries like Germany, France, Switzerland, and Hungary, the bishops of the Catholic Church openly rejected the Reformation and remained within the Catholic Church. In these countries the dissenters had no alternative but to form their own national churches; these they based upon a presbyterian form of government in which bishops no longer were permitted to rule— they reverted to the polity of the synagogue.

To this day, the synagogue has retained its democratic

form of religious government; the ownership and management of each synagogue is vested in the members of each congregation. Jewish congregations are generally administered by boards of trustees or governors who are duly elected according to the specific constitutional bylaws which are enacted autonomously by each congregation on its own. These men are responsible to the general membership in all matters relating to the program of the congregation. The rabbi is generally a member of the board of management, ex officio, and his advice and counsel are often sought in matters which relate to all phases of the congregation's activities. However, he holds no veto power; he exercises authority by virtue of his moral influence and scholarship, rather than by any legal or divine right. Congregations are free to elect their own rabbi for any length of time which is mutually desired, and rabbis are under no compulsion to serve in a particular community for any specific period of time. They, like the congregations they serve, are free agents.*

Thus, the principle of voluntarism governs the relationship of synagogue and rabbi—an ancient Jewish principle, yet profoundly in consonance with the traditions of our modern democratic way of life.

---

*Beginning with the 1970s, women also were welcomed into the North American Jewish community for the first time as candidates for rabbinical ordination. In response to the growing influence of religious feminists among non-Orthodox congregations, by 1984 liberal rabbinical seminaries had ordained close to one hundred women rabbis. In that year, too, the Jewish Theological Seminary of America agreed to open its doors to future women rabbis, who would, upon graduation, serve as the religious leaders of Conservative Jewish congregations. Orthodox rabbinical schools still refuse to ordain women, maintaining the traditional stance that only men are religiously qualified to act as the spiritual leaders of Jewish congregations.

# IV Symbols of Synagogue and Church Compared

The ways in which the symbols of the synagogue have influenced those of the church are many indeed. And yet a Christian who attends a synagogue service will find the visible signs of Jewish religious symbolism very few in number, and apparently dissimilar from those familiar to him from his own church.

As soon as one steps inside a synagogue, one becomes aware of its symbolical simplicity and its seeming lack of special design. Jewish law prescribes countless rules for the conduct of daily life, known as *mitzvot,* or commandments. Yet there are no directions given for the shape or form in which a synagogue should be built. Inside the sanctuary or chapel one does not find pictures, paintings, or sculpture. Because the synagogue is also a "house of study," there is only one indispensable object in it—a Scroll of the Law—which is read to the congregation at stated religious occasions. But it is not an object of adoration. A cabinet in which the Scroll is kept, known as *Aron Ha-Kodesh,* or Holy Ark, will also be found, and it will generally be on the eastern wall as a tribute to the importance of Jerusalem in Jewish history. The synagogue is thus "oriented" to the east and many churches still emulate this practice. The synagogue does not offer up sacrifices, not even symbolically, and therefore, instead of an altar, in the center of the dais we find a reader's desk, where the Scroll is placed when it is read to the congregation. In earlier times, as we have noted, the male members of the congregation read from the Scroll of the Torah at their own pews. Today the Torah is read by the Synagogue reader; the Scroll is kept at his desk, and various men are called forward to attend the reading at his side. The reading of the Torah and the lessons contained in it form a basic part of the service.

As a physical object the Torah itself is not holy; it has no inherent divine substance. The Jew believes, however, that its contents reflect the revelation of the will of God, and thus the synagogue has made the study of the Law a form of worship that is more important than prayer itself. Perhaps this is so because the leaders of the synagogue felt that when one prays, one tells God what is his own will; but when one studies the words of the Torah he learns what it is that God has willed. The synagogue in its form resembles a schoolhouse, or a forum, rather than a religious shrine, and this is a reflection of its function—to teach how one performs the *mitzvah,* the commandment of God.

Despite the basic simplicity of the prayer hall, there are some ritual symbols, particularly in modern synagogues, which are artistically embellished. The Scroll of the Law is encased in an embroidered cloth mantle; its wooden rollers may be adorned with silver crowns, and a silver breastplate and reading pointer are often strung across the mantle. A silk or velvet veil called a *parochet* generally covers the Torah Ark, and it may contain a variety of ornamental Biblical symbols. The *menorah,* or candlestick, is reminiscent of the ancient Temple and, in many congregations, is a veritable work of art. A perpetual light, called *ner tamid,* which hangs before the Torah Ark, is often embellished with artistic designs; it symbolizes the eternity of faith. But the purpose of the various ornamental designs and ritual art objects of the synagogue is not only to inspire a love of God, but to stimulate the congregation to perform the *mitzvah,* to fulfill the commandments of God by means of religious acts. For the Jew believes that in order to demonstrate the love of God, one must conform to His will.

We will soon learn the ways in which the Catholic and the Protestant Churches have retained some of the symbols of the synagogue, and observe, too, the ways in which they have branched off into their own unique directions. But before one can understand the differences between the symbols of synagogue and church, one must recognize that Christians and Jews *understand the symbols themselves in dramatically different ways.*

[36]

Jews and most Protestants see in a physical symbol an object that only suggests or recalls some worthy idea or event by reason of its relationship to that idea or event. A simple way to demonstrate this thought would be to think of what a national flag means to a patriot. It is a symbol that brings into focus all of the historical and patriotic associations of his nation. It is an *educational,* rather than a *mystical* symbol. But Catholics and a few Protestant denominations think of their major religious symbols as sacraments, or mysteries. Those symbols which many Christians consider to be sacraments become such, because it is believed that the Divine resides in them, and therefore the symbol itself partakes of the reality of God. For the Catholic, the sacrament is the physical embodiment of supreme mysteries. But for the Jews (as well as for many Protestants), the symbol is but a sign and a remembrance—an educational reminder, rather than a mystical experience.

*Some Christian Symbols Based on Jewish Background*

I BAPTISMAL FOUNT AND "MIKVAH"

The baptismal fount in the Catholic Church is placed near the Church entrance to remind Catholics that Baptism is the opening step in the sacramental way to the Christian life. It is derived from the ancient Jewish ritual bath known as the *mikvah,* which in Hebrew means a "gathering of water," and which came to be used as a description of a plunge, or ritual bath. The Hebrew Bible requires Israelites to take a purifying bath to remove ritual impurities which result from various kinds of physical uncleanliness. The ritual ablution had to take place in running water—usually a river—or in rainwater accumulated in pits or cavities. After the fall of the Temple, when the synagogue became the central Jewish religious institution, the *mikvah* was often built as part of the synagogue building, or placed in the courtyard of the synagogue. It was built to hold a minimum of two cubic yards or about two hundred gallons of water—enough to cover the entire human body. Before converts to Judaism could be officially accepted into the community, they had to undergo the ritual of immersion (or baptism), which usually took place in the *mikvah*. Baptism, in the Christian religions, is the symbol of the beginning of Christian life; it is based upon a similar Jewish rite which consummated conversion. To this day converts to Judaism are still required, by Orthodox and Conservative rabbis, to undergo a ritual bath of immersion in the *mikvah*. Thus when Christians participate in the ceremony or the sacrament of Baptism, they are borrowing a Jewish ritual which found its way into Christianity as early as the time of one of its immediate forerunners, John the Baptist.

## II CHURCH ALTAR CLOTHS AND JEWISH SHROUDS

The ancient Temple, of course, possessed an altar on which the various sacrifices were made daily. In the synagogue, prayer has replaced sacrifice, and therefore it does not contain an altar. Thus, church altars find their significance in their relationship to the ancient Temple, rather than to the synagogue. In many Christian congregations, that part of the church which contains the altar is known as the sanctuary —corresponding to the "Holy of Holies" of the ancient Temple. In Catholic churches, the altar is covered with three cloths of linen. Here, too, is a link to the Jewish past: Jews, to this day, are buried in linen shrouds—for the Christian, the altar serves as a reminder of the death of his Savior; indeed, it is the symbol of the place where he was sacrificed. Thus, the linen cloth which covers the altar in a Christian church is borrowed from the Jewish practice connected with the burial of the dead.

## III CHURCH CANDELABRA AND THE MENORAH

In many churches candelabra are used as part of religious worship. Very often they consist of seven branches—a reminder of the seven-branched *Menorah* which had been used in the Temple Service in Jerusalem. Most synagogues still retain the *Menorah* as a symbol of their tie to the ancient Jewish past. However the synagogue is a substitute for, rather than a replica of, the Temple, and so the *Menorah* to be found in most synagogues today consists, as we have already pointed out, of six or eight branches.

In the Roman Catholic Church, a tabernacle is placed at the rear of the altar containing the bread and wine used in the Mass. Before this tabernacle a lamp fed with pure olive oil burns perpetually, similar to the "eternal light" which was kindled on the altar of the ancient Temple, and which was ordained in Hebrew Scriptures: "And thou shalt command the children of Israel, that they bring unto thee pure olive oil beaten for the light, to cause a lamp to burn continually" (Exod. 27:20). In the synagogue of today, the perpetual lamp, or *ner tamid,* is placed before the Holy Ark containing the Torah Scrolls, and most often it is fed by electrical power, rather than oil.

## IV FIRST AND SECOND LESSONS AND THE READING OF THE LAW

The Jewish Scroll of the Law consists of handwritten sheets of parchment which contain the Five Books of Moses, or the Pentateuch. The *Torah* service in the synagogue is added to the regular daily worship on Monday and Thursday mornings, to the services of Saturday morning and afternoon, as well as to the major festivals. In order to teach the Mosaic Law to the congregation, the rabbis of old required that at these services, lessons from the *Torah,* or Pentateuch, be included in the prayer service itself. By means of an ingenious arrangement, they divided the Five Books of Moses into fifty-four sections, known as *sidrot* (*sidrah,* singular). Each of these sections was to be read during the course of one week, thus enabling the congregation to begin with Genesis in the fall and to conclude with Deuteronomy twelve months later. In this fashion, the entire Five Books of Moses are read in the Synagogue in the course of each year. In addition to these readings from the Pentateuch, selections from the Prophets are included in the Sabbath and Festival Services, following the reading from the Scroll, this selection being called *Haftarah*. It is the *Haftarah* which lads of thirteen years of age read publicly on that Sabbath when they are called before the congregation to observe their coming of age—the *Bar Mitzvah,* but of this, more later.

Thus, when Protestants or Catholics, at their Sunday church service, read one or two lessons from Scripture, they are simulating the practice which originated in the synagogue. In many Christian churches, the first "lesson" is taken from the Old Testament, while the second is a "parallel" reading from the New Testament. One can readily see how the "two lessons" closely resemble the practice in the synagogue, where a portion of the Law, or *sidrah,* is read each Sabbath, followed by the "second lesson," the *Haftarah,* the "prophetic selection" which echoes one or more of the themes mentioned in the *sidrah* of the Pentateuch.

Indeed, there is much evidence that, in the early church, the Biblical selections used each Sunday paralleled those which were being read in the synagogue on the Sabbath before. The church had compiled four books which served as a guide to the ritual service. The first, the Antiphonary, contained all that was to be sung by the choir; its pages were filled with translations of Hebrew prayers used in the Temple and synagogue. The third book, known as the Lectionary, contained all the Scriptural lessons that were read in the Mass Sunday after Sunday, and it closely followed the Scriptural cycle which had been established in the synagogue. The reading of Scripture as a form of public instruction became one of the major functions of the synagogue. Jews call the synagogue *shul* (Yiddish for school), and in this simple appellation there is captured a whole philosophy of religion. While the Roman Church did take over some of the instructional aspects of the synagogue service, its public ritual was primarily based upon the sacrificial system of the Temple. Indeed, the Mass is still called "the sacrifice of the Mass."

V THE CROSS AND THE "STAR OF DAVID"

It should not be surprising to learn, therefore, that there is no single basic or central symbol to the Jewish religion which completely expresses the whole of Judaism. When Christians see the Cross, whether they merely pay reverence to it or actually adore it, they have before them an immediate, concrete summation of the total meaning of Christianity. "No cross, no Christianity"—thus Christian preachers have correctly stated over the centuries, for the essential mystery of Christian faith is centered upon the crucifixion; all other Christian values are derived from it. When Jews live in a Christian society, they, too, seem to require a single, simple symbol which denotes their religion. As a result, the so-called "Star of David" has become identified in the minds of most people as the characteristic symbol of Judaism. Actually, there is nothing intrinsically Jewish about this six-pointed star, despite the fact that it is referred to in Hebrew as *Magen David,* the shield of David. Examples of this selfsame six-pointed star can be found in many cultures besides the Hebrew. Indeed, world travelers will remember seeing it in many medieval churches of Europe, where it was intended to represent a Christian rather than a Jewish symbol—two triangles interlocking, forming a double trinity.

If one were to seek a basic symbol which could represent a comprehensive statement of the meaning of Judaism, the closest he could come would be the Torah Scroll itself. For, if without the Cross there would be no Christianity, surely without the Torah there could be no Judaism. For Judaism is profoundly centered on the idea of the Law of God as revealed in the Hebrew Bible. But this Law can find neither graphic portrayal nor physical embodiment, since it is not the Scroll of the Law itself, but its religious and ethical teachings which are holy.

Perhaps this is why the inner adornments of a synagogue are usually most austere and without benefit of symbolical treatment. Characteristically, Judaism fears that a symbol may become an image, and if this were to happen the essential spirituality of the Law would be violated. For, the Jew believes that the Law is not merely a symbol of life—it is life itself.

# v Language, Music and Dress

## *Language*

For Protestant Christians, culture is something that lies outside of the realm of religion. Each nation-state is the possesser of its own "cultural personality," untied and unbound to any transnational cultural association. Thus, one of the projects of the Protestant Reformation was to eliminate Latin as the "vernacular of the church," and the language of its liturgy, and to replace it with the various national tongues which reflected the autonomous cultures of the lands in which Protestants lived.

The universality of the Roman Catholic Church required a universal language which would help to promote the order, uniformity and harmony of its doctrines. Having different national languages within the church, Catholics feel, paves the way to the formation of national churches—an idea quite subversive to Catholic dogma.

Judaism, on the other hand, is an "evolving religious civilization of the Jewish people." Therefore their language of prayer, Hebrew, is the language which has reflected that civilization from the earliest days unto the present. The Jewish people, throughout their history, have been multilingual. They had been forced into dispersion, and wherever they migrated they adjusted to the life and the language of the new lands into which they came. Although they spoke the language of their adopted countries, they nevertheless retained a knowledge of and an appreciation for their own language —Hebrew. Thus when you enter an Orthodox or a Conservative congregation, you will not be surprised to find that most of the religious service is still conducted in the Hebrew language—the national tongue of the Jewish people. The sermons of course are preached in English, and a number of English readings have been added to assist those members of the congregation who lack facility in reading or comprehending the Hebrew language.

If you should happen to attend one of the major services of

the week such as the Sabbath morning service, you will hear the cantor leading the liturgy in Hebrew melody. The reader, too, chants the weekly Scriptural lesson from the Torah Scroll in the original Hebrew in much the same way that it was done in the synagogue, even before the time of Jesus. Each weekly Torah lesson, or *sidrah,* is divided into seven portions, and for each portion a different male member of the congregation is called up to the reading desk where the Torah is read. In the synagogue hardly anything is read in a declamatory style, for the Hebrew prayers, many of which are from the Psalms and other poetical parts of the Hebrew Scripture, are all chanted. Even the worshippers chant the prayers out loud as they join in worship. But this should not be surprising if you remember that the chanting of prayers and the intoning of poems and sacred texts is a very ancient custom which still survives in Judaism. Indeed, in this way each worshipper personally participates and is able to get the feeling and the rhythm of the words. In Reform Jewish congregations, because they are the products of western manners and forms, there is hardly any Hebrew in the service and the worshippers participate principally by means of responsive English readings which are led by the rabbi. Of late, more of these congregations are returning to some of the traditional forms, and cantors, who for a long time were not associated with such services, are again chanting the Hebrew parts of the liturgy.

Prayer in the Hebrew language functions for Jews in much the same way that Latin does for Roman Catholics, but for entirely different reasons. Hebrew is the national language of the Jewish people, and thus reflects its own universal civilization. No matter where Jews live, they are united to each other by the transcendental character of their own religious culture. It is not an accident of history that those Jewish communities which neglected the study of the Hebrew language led the way toward the total assimilation of Jews into the non-Jewish world, for the Hebrew language is infinitely more than a language of liturgy alone. Unlike Latin, it is not "dead," nor has it ever been dead. The study of the Bible led Jews to the development of the Mishnah, compiled in Palestine about the year 200 of the Christian Era. The Mishnah, which consists of a later codification of civil and religious law based upon the Mosaic legislation, was written in Hebrew, but students of language can easily demonstrate the virile growth of the Hebrew language from the time of the Bible through the period of the Mishnah. The language grew as the life changed, for it was not merely the language of the synagogue, but the language of the people as well. In medieval times, additional works of great writing were created by the Jews. Poetry, philosophy, law and even science were fostered in Jewish communities from the shores of the western Mediterranean to the Persian Gulf. The Hebrew language developed apace, once again reflecting its inner vitality and growth. And in modern times as well, there has been a virtual renaissance of Hebrew language and literature which has found its center in the new State of Israel, where of course Hebrew is one of the two official languages of that land, Arabic being the other.

Thus Jews pray in Hebrew, not because God understands no other language, or because it is the liturgical language of the synagogue, but rather because it is their language and it therefore molds the content as well as the form of Jewish thought. When Jewish children prepare for Jewish religious life, in the various religious schools which have been created by different communities, the foundation of the entire educational system is a knowledge of the Hebrew language. To be sure, many of the great religious works which Judaism has contributed to the world may be read and understood in translation; but no translation can replace the original. Much as a graduate student of Italian literature would want to be able to read and to understand *The Divine Comedy* in the language in which it was written, and not rely upon second-hand sources, so the Jew has always believed in the need to participate in his own religious life through the medium of the Hebrew language. What is more, Hebrew is for the Jew a much more integral part of his cultural heritage.

But quite apart from general cultural considerations, from a purely religious point of view, Hebrew is a necessary tool for the Jew. Since the congregation participates in the religious service to a great extent, one can understand why Jews have always insisted upon a rigorous religious educational program for their children, which includes the mastery of reading, writing, and comprehension of the Hebrew language and its sacred literature.

To achieve such educational goals, it becomes necessary for Jews who live outside of the State of Israel to foster bi-culturalism as a way of life. In all of the lands in which they live as citizens, and to which they owe political allegiance, they naturally participate in the general cultural life. But over and beyond such participation, their own religious life, based upon the Hebraic civilization, requires for its survival, an additional educational system in order to achieve the goal of bi-culturalism. Thus Jewish children, at an early age, are introduced to the study of Hebrew, to an examination of the Scripture in the original, and to cultural experiences which center in Hebrew language and literature. For the most part, these children receive this education in afternoon schools conducted by congregations or other Jewish associations, which supplement the general program of studies provided by civil authorities. A smaller number attend private Jewish "day schools" where, under Jewish sponsorship, children are given both their secular and their religious training in the same institution. By and large, children who attend the latter type of school are exposed to a more intensive program of Jewish studies than time allows for in the former type of school. It is interesting to note that in North America, in very recent years, the "Jewish day school" has grown by leaps and bounds in the metropolitan Jewish communities. While one cannot expect that the majority of Jewish children will receive this more intensive kind of instruction, the fact that the minority has grown is a clear indication of the greater emphasis which more Jewish parents are placing upon religious education. In an age when we speak of the "return to religion," attendance at worship services alone is not the chief guide or index to the intensity of the "return." The development of more comprehensive and intensive Jewish religious schools in the past several years is a surer guide and reflection of the growing religious spirit now abroad in the Jewish community. For Jews have never placed as much emphasis upon public worship as they have upon private study of religious texts and sources. Indeed, this has been the significant aspect of the title which they have borne: "The People of the Book."

## Music

Music, as everyone knows, has been intimately associated with organized religion just as many of the other arts have been. The music you will hear in the synagogue is based upon the cantillation of the Scripture and is different from the way in which music was used in the ancient Temple. The Temple employed a large priestly orchestra and a trained choir. Indeed, in the Book of Psalms mention is made of a large number of instruments which were used at the time of the Temple. But the synagogue never emulated the Temple in this, as it had in other ways, and so it frowned upon the use of instrumental music at its services. Indeed, after the destruction of the Temple, all instrumental music, even for religious purposes, was prohibited, as a sign of national mourning over the loss of the Temple. The synagogue *hazzan,* or cantor, was thus required to chant the liturgy without accompaniment, except for the congregational responses. Today, however, all Reform and some Conservative congregations have introduced the organ and mixed choir as a regular part of synagogue services.

The influence of synagogue music upon the Church was strong in the first seven Christian centuries, and during that period there was similar Christian hostility to instrumental music at the service. The early Church Fathers directed that only the human voice might be employed at divine services. To this day, this rule is still observed in the Oriental communities of Christendom—the Syriac, Jacobite, and Nestorian churches. The music of the Roman Catholic Church in the West has for many centuries been performed to the accompaniment of choirs and instrumentalists. Yet, when one listens to the priest chanting the liturgy of the Mass, he cannot fail to recognize that it is in the mode of the music of the synagogue. As one Church authority has put it: "The Gregorian chant is the music of the Hebrews."

## Dress

One of the very first distinguishing marks that greets the stranger upon entering an Orthodox or Conservative synagogue is the unusual sight of men worshipping with their heads covered, wearing hats or skull-caps. This is another custom that has come out of the East. It is a reminder, once again, that Judaism had its origin in the land of Palestine, and that, through all these years, it still bears many of the hallmarks of the East. For while we cannot very easily ascribe a single, simple reason as being responsible for this custom, which has become a hallowed tradition among Jews, we do know that it is in part due to the manners and customs of the eastern world. Western man raises his hat in respectful greeting, but the Near East is accustomed to doing just the opposite. For an Oriental to appear bareheaded before his guests is a breach of good manners which would be deeply resented. This conventional gesture of politeness towards one's fellow men eventually must have become a sign of awe and respect in the presence of God, and it took on all the aspects of a

sacred custom. Moreover, the High Priest of old, when officiating in the Jerusalem Temple, was distinguished by a miter
made of fine linen cloth, which was coiled around his head
like a turban. A diadem of pure gold was fastened to it with
a purple cord and it bore the inscription: "Holiness unto the
Lord," a phrase summarizing the aim and the purpose of his
office. When the Temple was destroyed, the office of the High
Priest ceased to exist and thereafter the distinction between
priesthood and laity became obsolete in Judaism. It is probable that the head-covering of the Jews at prayer has some
relationship to this historical situation. Once the High Priest
wore a miter on his head; now the people, having, so to
speak, assumed the priestly role, wear miters as an act of
symbolic remembrance.

Women appeared veiled in the early synagogue and
church. The veil was also a kind of headgear, and that is why
to this day women do not enter a synagogue or a Catholic
church without some kind of head-covering, even if they wear
only flowers in their hair. In Orthodox synagogues women
are seated in a separate section, as was the custom in the
ancient Temple. Conservative and Reform congregations in
North America have introduced family pews as a modifica-
tion of the old tradition, in deference to the democratic character of new world society—granting women a measure of
equality.

In the Catholic Church there are still some vestiges of
the Jewish custom of men covering their heads at prayer.
Throughout the Middle Ages the fashionable nobles wore
hats in church, and when the solemn prayers were recited
they did not doff their hats, but pushed them to the back of
their elaborate coiffures. Since, in the West, it was thought to
be irreverent to don a hat during prayers, the Catholic clergy
adopted the custom of covering their heads during the less
solemn moments, and of doffing their headgear during the
more sacred parts of the service. In this connection, it is of
some interest to mention a special privilege Pope Paul V

(1605–1621) granted to the Catholic missionaries in China. The regular discipline of the Catholic Church permits the clergy to wear a *beretta* (from the Latin word *birrus,* which means a cape or hood) only during the less solemn moments of the Mass, as previously mentioned. The *beretta* is a square cap with three corners rising from the crown, possibly suggestive of the three parts of the Trinity. Cardinals wear red *berettas* and all clergy below this rank wear black ones. But, because in China, it was considered indecent to appear in public with the head uncovered, the clergy were permitted to keep their *berettas* on throughout the entire Mass. From this practice, one can readily see the significance that eastern cultures attach to the covering of the head in public places.

There is still another kind of head-covering worn by the Catholic clergy. This is the *zucchetto,* from the Italian word, *zuccha,* which means a gourd. It is a small, closely fitting skull-cap, shaped like a saucer and of a red, violet, or black color, according to the rank of the wearer. That worn by the cardinal is always red. Cardinal red symbolizes that these select clergy must be ready to defend the rights of the Pope even unto the shedding of blood. The Pope, we should add, wears neither a *beretta* nor a *zucchetto.* He uses, instead, a tight-fitting cap, always white in color, called a *solideo,* which means "only to God," from the Latin *solus* and *deus.* He doffs it only to God during the more solemn parts of the Mass, but never at any other time. The rest of the clergy may wear black *zucchettos,* except for archbishops and bishops who wear violet ones. The miter of the bishop, which is donned and doffed at the Mass is, of course, a direct descendant of the headgear of the High Priest of Jerusalem. Except for the Episcopalians and Anglicans, Protestant clergy and laymen do not use any headgear at sacred services. Since Protestantism was conceived in the West, it is perfectly understandable why this should be.

Besides the head-covering, there is a second article of dress which is most striking to the stranger in the synagogue.

This item, like the head-covering, is worn in Orthodox and Conservative but not in Reform congregations. It is called a *tallit,* or prayer shawl, and it is worn by adult males, although younger boys may often also wear it at services. The *tallit* resembles the style of an outer garment worn in ancient Palestine. In time, when Jews lived outside of Palestine and adopted other garments for dress, the *tallit* was set aside just for ritual purposes. Its religious or ritual significance is especially related to the fringes or *tzitzit* at each of its four corners. This is in accordance with the Biblical prescription to "make . . . a fringe upon the corners of their garments . . . that you may look upon it and remember the commandments of the Lord." In early times these fringes were worn on the outer garments, and were a distinguishing mark of the Jews, who, even by means of their dress, desired to recall the commandments of God in the daily pursuit of life. Later on, perhaps because of their fear of persecution, instead of wearing the fringe on the outer garments, they placed it on a small undergarment. To this day, devout Jewish men wear this *arba kanfot,* or "four corners," as an undergarment every day of their lives. The fringe, which is a symbol and a reminder of the commandments, was later adapted from this undergarment and placed upon the prayer shawl, which Jewish men wear at every morning service, whether at home or in the synagogue. Since the rabbi and the cantor are essentially laymen and not priests, they, too, wear the same kind of prayer shawl at the synagogue service. In Conservative and Reform congregations, it has become the custom for those who lead the services to wear a black pulpit robe in addition to the cap and prayer shawl. In Orthodox congregations, usually only the cantor wears such a robe. But the robe is merely a matter of outer form and has no intrinsic religious significance.

In certain Protestant churches, the "Jewish prayer shawl," in the form of a clerical stole is worn by the officiating clergy during worship services. Roman Catholic priests wear six different sacred vestments in celebrating Mass—all of which are derived from ancient Jewish sources. Seeing a priest in this dress, one gets a better idea of what the officiants in the Jewish Temple of Jerusalem wore at their service. In the twenty-eighth chapter of the Book of Exodus, and the eighth chapter of the Book of Leviticus, detailed descriptions of the vestments of the priests of ancient Israel are given. Nowadays, in Catholicism, only the Pope wears a stole in daily life, as evidence of his special position. In the earlier Christian Church all priests wore a stole which, like the *tallit,* enveloped the entire body; then, like the Jewish High Priest, they had bells placed on the bottom edges of the garment, so that laymen might hear them coming and stand in awe before their presence.

While the church borrowed many of these specifically Jewish procedures, the language, music, and vestments of the synagogue still retain a character all their own. The use of Hebrew is a reminder of the ongoing religious civilization of the Jewish people which is reflected still in the prayer services of the congregation. The music of the synagogue echoes with the cadences of its oriental background: one can still hear in the overtones of the cantillation, the sounds which reverberated in the dwellings and market places of ancient Near Eastern communities. The outward religious garb, the prayer shawl, and head-covering, are living vestiges of the Semitic attire in the ancient Fertile Crescent.

In the synagogue then, these visible and audible signs of Jewish antiquity are a dramatic reminder of the survival of this people from earliest times.

# v*a* Sacred Texts

## *Bible*

The Bible, of course, is not the same book for all the religious faiths. All three groups use different "authorized" [English] translations: Most Jews use the translation prepared by the Jewish Publication Society; Catholics use the Douay Bible and the Revised Standard Version—Catholic Edition; Protestants use the King James Version, the New English Bible, or the Revised Standard Version. Jewish Scripture consists of what is called the Old Testament. This is a veritable library comprising thirty-nine books, divided into three parts: the Law, or Pentateuch; the Prophets; and the Writings. From the point of time, they cover the life of the Jewish people over a period of two thousand years. The canonization of the Law took place about 400 B.C.E.; the books of the Prophets were canonized two hundred years later. The third section, the Writings, was closed about the year 90 C.E.

Christians refer to Jewish Scripture as the Old Testament because they see their own Scripture, the New Testament, as fulfilling and surpassing it. Indeed, there was a time in the early Church when some Christians sought to cast out the Jewish Bible entirely, and Marcion of Rome was the leader of just such a movement. But others felt that without the Jewish Scripture there could be no real validation for the Christian belief in a Messiah. In their view, Jewish sacred writings were necessary, as a justification of their new faith. Marcion's opponents prevailed, and all Christians, to this day, include the Old Testament as part of their Bible.

Marcion's strictures against the so-called Old Testament must have given some impetus to the compiling of the various religious writings of the Christians. After having been edited and brought together, these were canonized in the middle of the second century. When this happened, these Christian writings became a New Testament, which the Church now believed supplemented and outranked the Old, but which could not ever displace it.

While the Jews of Palestine limited the contents of their Scripture to the books we know as the Old Testament, the Greek-speaking Jews who lived in Egypt did not stop there. They used a Greek translation of the Hebrew Bible, known as the Septuagint. This version of the Bible contained a number of books which were not considered holy by the Jews of Palestine. The early Church used the Septuagint as its Bible, since it was concerned, on the whole, with Greek-speaking pagans and Jews. In this way, these additional books, known as the Apocrypha, or "outside books," entered into the Church version of the Old Testament, while they were kept outside of the Bible of the synagogue. The Apocrypha appears scattered throughout the Old Testament of the early Church and remains that way even in the Vulgate, the Latin translation of the Bible produced by St. Jerome, at the end of the fourth century. Indeed, this still remains the official arrangement of the Catholic version of the Old Testament. Luther's translation of the Bible, on the other hand, kept the books of the Old Testament in one section and placed the Apocrypha in the middle, followed by the books of the New Testament. Within Protestantism there was a growing sentiment to follow the official Palestinian arrangement of the Old Testament. Finally, in the nineteenth century, the Apocrypha was removed from the Protestant Bible entirely, and only the Old and New Testaments were kept.

We have already noted the manner in which the Five Books of Moses, or Pentateuch, are integrated into the regular Sabbath morning services throughout the year. But synagogue worship goes much farther in attempting to incorporate even more Bible readings into the order of service. From the Books of the Prophets, a different selection is chanted each Sabbath. Five complete Biblical books, known as the *megillot,* or scrolls, are read in their entirety on special occasions: *Ecclesiastes* on the Sabbath of *Sukkot; Esther* on *Purim*, the Feast of Lots; *Song of Songs* on the Sabbath of Passover; *Ruth* on *Shavuot,* the Feast of Weeks; and *Lam-*

*entations,* on the Ninth Day of Av. At the Day of Atonement service, the whole Book of Jonah, with its universal teachings, is read to the congregation. Thus, while not all of the Bible's thirty-nine books are included in the synagogue services, the Pentateuch is read completely and each of the other two divisions of Scripture, the Prophets and the Writings are very well represented. Moreover, in traditional Jewish homes, during the week which follows the death of a member of the family, it is customary for the mourners to read aloud from the Psalms as well as from the Book of Job.

The Hebrew Bible is known affectionately as *TaNak,* the three consonants representing the first letters of the words by which the three divisions are called: *T*orah (Pentateuch), *N*eviim (Prophets), *K*etuvim (Writings). The order of these divisions, together with their component books, follows:

# I TORAH

*Genesis*
*Exodus*
*Leviticus*
*Numbers*
*Deuteronomy*

# II NEVIIM

[a] *Joshua*
   *Judges*
   I *Samuel*
   II *Samuel*
   I *Kings*
   II *Kings*

[b] Major Prophets
   *Isaiah*
   *Jeremiah*
   *Ezekiel*

[c] The Twelve
   Minor Prophets
   *Hosea*
   *Joel*
   *Amos*
   *Obadiah*
   *Jonah*
   *Micah*
   *Nahum*
   *Habakkuk*
   *Zephaniah*
   *Haggai*
   *Zechariah*
   *Malachi*

## III KETUVIM

> *Psalms*
> *Proverbs*
> *Job*
> *Song of Songs*
> *Ruth*
> *Lamentations*
> *Ecclesiastes*
> *Daniel*
> *Ezra*
> *Nehemiah*
> I *Chronicles*
> II *Chronicles*

When Scripture is read in the synagogue, it is customary for the congregation to follow the recitation closely by referring to the text, in the Bibles provided for each worshipper. But many worshippers go beyond the reading of the text alone. They cross-reference the text with traditional Hebrew commentaries which illumine the meaning of the verses and amplify them. The favorite and most beloved of these medieval Biblical commentaries still in vogue among Jews is that written by an eleventh-century scholar who lived in northern France, known affectionately as *Rashi*. *Rashi* was a rabbi, because he had been ordained by his teachers to teach and to interpret the Law. His vocation, however, was that of vintner, and his public teaching and training of future scholars was done as a labor of love. His commentaries cover virtually all of the books of the Hebrew Bible and are characterized by a compactness of style, and a close adherence to the literal meaning of the text. When he was in doubt as to whether his students would understand certain Hebrew terms, he translated the phrases, using Hebrew letters, into medieval French. As a result, hundreds of Gallicisms, idiomatic French expressions of the early Middle Ages, have been preserved in *Rashi's* commentaries, and students of the history of the French language have relied upon him for much information regarding the history and development of that tongue. *Rashi's* Biblical commentary also had an indirect impact upon Christianity, for Nicholas de Lyra, a fourteenth century Christian Bible student, relied upon this exegesis most heavily—and it was de Lyra's commentaries, in turn, upon which Martin Luther was most dependent when he made his monumental translation of Scripture into the German language. Many other medieval Christian Bible commentators and translators, too, were clearly indebted to the lucid and authoritative scholarship of *Rashi's* Biblical interpretations.

## Siddur, The Prayer Book

The traditional Hebrew prayer book has a long and colorful history, containing elements that stretch over three thousand years. Obviously, then, it is not the work of one man but, like the Hebrew Bible, it is a reflection of the unfolding development of the Jewish people on its own land and in several diaspora communities.

The single largest source for the Prayer Book is the Psalms, which cover a history of close to a thousand years, beginning as early as David (1000 B.C.E.) down to the time of the Second Temple. The Hebrew Psalter, consisting of 150 psalms, is often referred to as "the hymn-book of the Second Temple," because it was during the time that this Temple stood that the priests and Levites performed their rituals to the musical accompaniment of these inspiring and pious songs of praise.

It was not until the ninth century, however, that the first complete *siddur* was compiled and edited. Rabbi Amram, head of the Academy at Sura, Babylonia, seat of the foremost Jewish religious authority of the time, was responsible for this. In addition to the Biblical material, he incorporated the prayers and benedictions which the rabbis of the Talmud had written, and which had become part of the accepted traditional pattern. The structure of most services was built around the *Shema* (Hear, O Israel . . .) and the *Amiôah*, a prayer of silent devotion containing nineteen Benedictions, erroneously called the "Eighteen," which contains but one prayer for personal prosperity and sustenance. The *Siddur* is exceptionally free from personal petition, for the Hebrew language of prayer concentrates upon the plural, rather than the singular, the group, rather than the individual. Indeed, the rabbis of the Talmud ordained that on the Sabbath and Festivals it was improper to offer petitions to God which revolved about private wants or needs—only the welfare of the group may be mentioned on those occasions.

The core of the *Siddur* is still the Psalter, and the "Book of Common Prayer" of the Anglican, Episcopal, and other Protestant churches, not to mention the Roman Catholic Missal, were also shaped and influenced by the Psalms. (Indeed, the Rosary, among Catholics, while dedicated to Mary, is based upon Psalms, for the complete Rosary consists of 150 beads, divided into 15 sections of ten each—to correspond to the 150 Psalms of Hebrew Scripture.) Even the idiom of prayer in the Christian Church is often a direct borrowing from the Hebrew tradition. The familiar and basic prayer, "Our Father" (Paternoster), uses the plural form of petition—give *us,* forgive *us,* deliver *us,*—just as it is done in the synagogue. The idea of the "Kingdom of God" is a Hebrew phrase and concept, and comes into the Christian service straight out of the synagogue prayer book. The "Lord's Prayer" is a shortened form of five of the original six of the "Eighteen Benedictions" found in the Hebrew prayer book, while the Sermon on the Mount is a terse summary of basic Pharisaic doctrine, and many of its ideas and phrases have been part of the synagogue service since the very beginning of its history. The *Shema*—Hear, O Israel, the Lord our God, the Lord is One (Deut. 6:4), is the central prayer of the synagogue, and the verses which immediately follow have been hallowed for centuries. The love of God with all one's heart, might, and soul, as well as the command to love one's neighbor as one's self (Lev. 19:18), which form an important and pivotal Christian prayer and teaching, are not only taken from the Hebrew Bible, but also have been echoed in the synagogue service for centuries. Even the Hebrew language itself is still spoken at church worship whenever clergy or congregation use these words, all borrowed from the synagogue prayer book: Hallelujah, Selah, Amen.

*Siddur* is the Hebrew word for prayer book, and it means "order." This reflects the highly liturgical and formal character of synagogue worship. Each day of the year, at least three services are recited—morning, afternoon and evening. The morning service may be recited any time after dawn until noon, the afternoon service from shortly after noon until dusk, and the evening service any time after sunset. For practical purposes, most synagogues arrange the daily morning service sometime before 9:00 A.M., to enable the worshippers to arrive at work at a reasonable hour. Similarly, the afternoon and evening services are usually said successively, just before the sun sets, and immediately following its setting, to facilitate matters. Reform temples, however, have generally deleted daily services from their programs, and concentrate primarily on Friday evening and Sabbath morning worship.

The prayers for each service are clearly established and arranged in the prayer book, and from one synagogue to another (except Reform) there will be hardly any deviation. By and large, these services are conducted by the lay members of the congregation themselves, who act as their own cantors. On the yearly anniversary of a parent's death (*Yahrzeit*), it has become customary for the son to attend the three daily services, beginning with the evening before, and in addition to reciting the *Kaddish,* to serve as the cantor, as a ritual tribute to the memory of the deceased.

As a result of this close relationship to both the conduct of the prayer services and the contents of the prayer book, the *Siddur* has become an intimately-known book to the devoted Jewish worshipper. Next to the Bible, the *Siddur*, which consists of so many quotations from Scripture, is the most beloved text of the synagogue.

## The Talmud

On summer Sabbath afternoons, when the days are longer and afford greater opportunity for study and reflection, the synagogue study circles devote themselves to an analysis of the "Ethics of the Fathers." This six-chapter compendium of law, lore, and moral dicta is one of the products of the Pharisaic teachers, the ancient rabbis and their Talmudic academies. It has actually been incorporated into the Prayer Book. Jews are expected to study the Bible, the Prayer Book, as well as the Talmud and its commentaries.

The Talmud, which is not a book, but a vast literature, is the collective work of many generations of scholars and teachers. It consists of more than six thousand large folio pages whose contents were filled over a period of almost one thousand years, from about four hundred before and five hundred after the Christian Era. There are references in it to more than two thousand scholars who participated in its deliberations—men who lived principally in Palestine or Babylonia.

In more ancient days in Judaism, oral teachings, the unwritten traditions which each generation handed down to the next, were not supposed to be committed to writing. Perhaps this was done, so as not to allow any other book or books to rival the Bible—the written Law—in importance. But with the passage of time it became impossible for any one man to master the whole body of Oral Teaching, because of the expanded nature of the Talmudic literature. By the year two hundred of the Christian Era, the Mishnah, a first code, was put into writing and edited in Palestine by Rabbi Judah the Prince. Despite the fact that most Jews of this period no longer used Hebrew in daily speech, but employed another Semitic tongue, Aramaic, instead, the Mishnah maintains an unbroken line with the Biblical past, and is therefore written in Hebrew.

It is interesting to note, however, that the compilers of the Mishnah coined many new Hebrew words to express ideas and situations which were not recorded in Biblical Hebrew, in much the same way that the Hebrew language in the modern State of Israel has continued to grow with the needs of contemporary life. But the language is the same language and the addition of new word forms only gives testimony to its living qualities. Alas, such linguistic continuity does not obtain in any other of the ancient cultures: Modern Egyptians speak Arabic, and not Egyptian; Italians do not speak Latin; nor do modern Greeks speak the language of Homer.

This first code, the Mishnah, together with the Torah-law, became the basic legal text of the schools in Palestine and Babylonia. About the year 500 C.E., a second code, actually a commentary on and a further amplification of the Mishnah was edited. This code, known as the *Gemara,* was written mainly in Aramaic, with only a small amount of Hebrew. The Gemara was compiled in two editions—one in Palestine, the other in Babylonia; the Babylonian being the more important of the two. The Babylonian Gemara together with the Mishnah make up the Talmud—which is the basic repository of Jewish law and religious thought as developed and interpreted by the rabbis until the year 500. Since then, subsequent generations of Jewish scholars have made the Talmud a special subject of inquiry and knowledge and have added to its insights and judgments by writing numerous commentaries and treatises based upon its teachings. Indeed, before men are ordained as rabbis, they are expected to be

[61]

masters of Talmudic literature, and thus qualified to render decisions based upon authentic rabbinical sources.

Hardly an aspect of life escapes the notice of the Talmudic teachers, and rabbinic law becomes co-extensive with the whole of living. A broad concern for the total human being is revealed in the pages of the Talmud, which goes far beyond mere ritual or ecclesiastical regulations. In this sense, it is a continuation of the Hebrew Bible which similarly reveals an unremitting interest in the daily personal and social habits of men, in their espousal of social justice, and in the development of their ethical nature. This is why, in Hebrew, Talmudic law is also known as *Halakah,* for it is taken from the Biblical phrase which defines religion as the ability to "walk in the ways of God." *Halakah* is not a manner of speech, nor a style of praying, but a "way of life."

In traditional synagogues, special study halls, equipped with Talmudical libraries containing numerous reference works, are made available to all members of the community. Even the smallest of these congregations will rarely fail to be the proud possessor of a formidable library which often contains old and rare editions dealing with the ethics, jurisprudence, theology, and philosophy of Judaism. The Beth Hamidrash, or "house of study" of each of the synagogues, is considered to be its treasure center. For while the commandment prohibiting graven images has precluded pictorial art from the synagogue, it has made no stipulation against books; indeed it has welcomed such repositories of ideas.

In the Talmud there is a teaching which says: "If all the other of the 613 Commandments were placed on one balance, and only the 'commandment to study' were placed on the other, the latter would outweigh the former."

More than prayer, then, it is study—the search for truth and the development of an inquiring mind—which makes the synagogue a sacred place.

[62]

*PART II* SACRED MOMENTS

# VI Birth

From cradle to grave a man's religion follows him. From time immemorial he has approached the significant days of his life with special feeling and concern. Birth, puberty, marriage, and death are all such moments. Primitive man attempted to appease the wrath of the gods at such occasions, by offering sacrifices of the most precious things he possessed: a child, an animal, or the bounties of his crop. With the passage of time the idea of ethical monotheism developed as a way of life for many peoples. But man continued to remain a man and not a god. He still felt the need of being a part of a power greater than himself. And this need was and is especially strong at moments of physical crisis, when, despite all that man imagines he can accomplish on his own, he comes to recognize his own frailty. These crisis periods in human life are related to man's birth, growth, and death. That is why, although its customs will vary, every ancient or modern culture has developed special rites of significance that accompany man through these important moments of physical insecurity, *rites de passage*. Although related by the very nature of the physical crisis, the customs of each group vary. These differences teach us a great deal about the attitudes the group takes toward the whole of life.

It is our purpose to examine each of these moments in human life to see how Jews face them, and then to examine some vestiges of Jewish practice which have been retained by Christians.

For Christians, the church is the focal point of every personal religious commemoration. For Jews, the synagogue is a sacred place, but not *the* sacred place. Above the synagogue is the Law, and it reaches far beyond the synagogue walls. So it is that when a male child is born to a Jewish family, the rituals that accompany the first days of life take place outside of the synagogue. Jewish law, based upon Scripture, definitely prescribes: "And on the eighth day the flesh of his foreskin shall be circumcised." Whatever the origin of this rite, circumcision has been and still is one of the most basic of

[65]

Jewish *mitzvot*. In Hebrew, this ritual is known as *b'rit,* and this means covenant or agreement. Its very name, therefore, suggests its deep meaning to the Jew. It signifies that from Abraham's time forward, the Jewish people believed that they had made a pact with God, to live in accordance with laws and beliefs that clearly marked them out as a separate people. Circumcision is a sign of the covenant, and it is a kind of religious initiation, on the eighth day after birth, into membership in the community of Israel. The rite is performed by a Jewish functionary, known as the *mohel,* or circumciser, and may take place at home, or in the hospital. The ritual of circumcision confers no new status upon a child born of a Jewish mother, nor does its omission deny such a child specific religious benefits. (A male child whose father is Jewish, but whose mother is not, would be required, according to Jewish law, to be circumcised, in order to be deemed Jewish.) At the time of the circumcision, the child is given a Hebrew name, usually one borne by some deceased relative. This is the name he will use whenever he participates in Jewish religious ceremonies which require it, such as Bar Mitzvah or marriage. Indeed, this ritual not only symbolizes the beginning of life, but also of a Jewish way of life. For, when the father recites a blessing of thanks for the privilege of inducting his child into the "covenant of Abraham," all the guests assembled at this festive occasion sound its theme. They recite together from the ritual: "As he entered the covenant, so may he live to study the Torah, to be wedded, and to live a life of good deeds."

If the child is also the first-born son of his mother, still another ceremony is conducted when he is thirty-one days old. In early Jewish history, the Law required that first-born males be dedicated to the service of God. They were Israel's first priests. Later, Aaron and his descendants were chosen to replace the firstborn as priests. But a religious rite developed which required that first-born males, as a reminder of the role of their ancestors, undergo a "ritual of release" from their service to God on the thirty-first day of life. In observant Jewish families this ceremony is still conducted. A person, known as a *Kohen* because he traces his lineage to the priestly family of Aaron, acts as the officiant. The father brings the baby before him and gains the child's "release," by making a symbolic gift offering to God, consisting of five "shekels." Generally, five half-dollar pieces are used. The *Kohen* then invokes the priestly blessing of Aaron upon the child and returns the five "shekels" to the parents, who then contribute the money to some charity. Today, this ceremony has lost its original meaning because there is no longer the institution of a priesthood in Judaism. However, many families still observe this rite as a reminder of the ancient laws, and as a bond to the historic ways of the Jewish people. Implied in the ceremony, too, is the idea that new life comes from God, and children have only been "loaned" to their parents.

For new-born girls there is a simple ceremony which is conducted as part of the regular synagogue service. Special prayers for the well-being of the sick, or for personal gratitude on recovery from illness, are recited in the synagogue at the time the Torah is read. When this portion of the service is reached, the father of the girl is called to the reading desk, and after reciting the usual benediction over the Torah, he offers a special prayer for the health of the mother and child. They are not present at this service, for the father usually comes to the synagogue on the very first Sabbath after the birth. As part of the special prayer, the girl is given a Hebrew name, and she, like a boy, will use it for religious ceremonies in the future. After the service, the happy event is celebrated at home by the family and their friends.

Birth is an extremely important occasion in Jewish religious life. Through prayer, it is a time of thanksgiving. It is also a time of induction, a moment of formal entry into the ranks of a people dedicated to a unique way of life. But for the Jew, the various rituals which surround birth do not provide the child with any mystical armor or spiritual grace. The reader will recall our earlier discussion of baptism as a culminating ritual of Jewish conversion. Christians have taken this Jewish ceremony of baptism and given it specific Christian meaning—in many churches it has been endowed with sacramental significance. This means that baptism for many Christians is an outward sign of an inward and invisible grace which helps to change the nature of the child or the adult who is baptized. For many Christians, baptism has been made into a religious requirement for the salvation of the soul. While traditional Judaism asks that the convert be fully immersed in water as an outward sign of purification from heathen ways, the earlier Christians did, and the Roman Catholics still do, require the pouring of water over the head—an outward sign of the inner and invisible change that takes place—the cleansing of original or actual sin.

In the case of Catholic children, parents bring the newborn baby to church within the first month of its life. This is usually done on a Sunday afternoon, when the parents, and the godparents chosen by them, bring the child to the priest. He takes a small pitcher filled with specially blessed baptismal water and pours it on the baby's head three times. Since the child is also given a "Christian" name at this time, baptism has also come to be known as christening. This custom is probably derived from the Jewish practice of naming boys at circumcision. Indeed, in the early Church there was often doubt whether, in view of the Jewish practice of "eighth day circumcision," any day earlier than the eighth was permissible for Christian baptism.

Some Protestant churches broke away from others mainly because of a difference in their views on baptism. These denominations base themselves on the idea of a "gathered church." In other words, they believe that those who join the church must do so out of a personal desire and will to join, and out of their own understanding. Thus, the church is "gathered together" by those who are converted to it. Since baptism was originally a Jewish ritual of conversion, these churches believe that they have retained its early meaning when they insist that baptism is for those who have reached an age of understanding, and are thus "converting" to the church. Moreover, since it is a symbol of the washing away of sin, they believe that it can only be undertaken by those old enough to know what sin means. For these reasons, they wait until the child is twelve years or older, when, after religious instruction, he may be expected to know what it means to accept the Christian faith. Many of these same groups also perform baptism in the ancient Jewish way—by complete immersion. Often, they have baptisteries, or small pools, built into their churches, where this rite is performed, while still others may use some running stream for the performance of the ceremony.

Thus, some of the ancient Jewish rites of conversion have been retained among Christians to this day. Baptism, whether it takes place immediately following birth or at some later period in life, whether Catholic or Protestant, is a ceremony or a sacrament which goes back to an earlier Jewish practice. But since Jews constitute a people rather than a church, the very fact that one has been born into a Jewish family automatically makes him part of the Jewish community. Thus, the rites which surround the birth of a Jewish person are not so much initiatory in character as they are covenantal. The Jewish people consider themselves chosen by God to serve as the Messiah people, to teach the world the meaning of the Moral Law. Thus, a child born unto a Jewish mother is, by the very act of birth, already a Jew: he needs no further induction ceremony. The religious rites which follow his birth are not intended to confer upon him the status of a Jew (although sociologically speaking, in practice, they have done this), as much as they are designed to symbolize the covenant of the Jew with the God of Israel. Abraham is considered to have been a Jew even before he made his covenant with God to serve Him by becoming the father of His people. But the act of circumcision which Abraham performed upon himself and the members of his family, inducted them into a relationship with God, individually and collectively, making his people into B'nai B'rith—the people of the covenant. Thus, from the very first days in the life of a Jew, his unique status as a member of a unique people, is indelibly borne in upon him.

# VII Puberty

In the Hebrew Bible the age of responsibility is considered to be twenty. When a man reached that age he was thought to be an adult. But obviously, between his birth and maturity, some special ceremonies must have been celebrated. We do not know too much about what rites were performed during his teens. But beginning at least six hundred years ago, a religious event was observed during a boy's thirteenth year. This has come to be known as the *Bar Mitzvah,* when a boy becomes a child of the commandments. We shall see how this event is related to the blessings recited during the first days of his life, at the time of circumcision, when family and friends prayed: "May he live to study and observe the Torah."

But before we tell of *Bar Mitzvah* we should mention a custom that grew up among the people which sheds light upon the relationship of parents to their children and the Torah. On *Shavuot* (The Feast of Weeks), which commemorates the giving of the Torah at Sinai, parents brought their little boys to the synagogue wrapped in a prayer shawl. There they were blessed by the rabbi before the Scroll of the Torah, and the section containing the Ten Commandments was read to them. Afterward, they were taken into the religious school for their very first lesson. As part of the lesson, honey was smeared on a slate to spell out one of the verses from Scripture. The children were then told to taste the honey. The adults assembled offered the hope that the words of the Torah would be sweet to their taste, like honey. This quaint custom has been adapted in many modern North American Jewish congregations into what is called a "Consecration Service." A short time after young boys and girls are enrolled for the first time in the congregational religious school, a special service is dedicated to their new career as "children of the Torah," and the blessing of God is invoked upon them.

From the day the child enters the religious school, his education consists of discovering what it means to be a member of the Jewish people. A basic part of this training deals with the Law and the commandments, which provide the pattern for daily religious conduct. Until a boy is thirteen years of age, he is not responsible for observing all of these rules; his father bears the responsibility for him. But after he has been schooled in the religious ways of the Jewish people, he is expected to conduct his life in accordance with them. The source of this special way of life stems from the Torah, and that is why, on his thirteenth birthday, the ceremony of *Bar Mitzvah* revolves about the Torah. On the day of his *Bar Mitzvah,* he is called to the Torah for the first time, like any other adult male. Sometimes he acts as the reader of the congregation on that day and publicly chants the weekly Scriptural lesson. Most often, he will only read the weekly selection from the Prophets, or the *Haftarah*. The *Bar Mitzvah* ceremony almost always takes place at the Sabbath morning service, although it could conceivably be held at any service where the Torah is read. The rabbi usually charges the boy with his new responsibilities after the young man has finished his ritual.

Earlier, we pointed out that the religious rites at birth do not confer Jewish status as much as they symbolize the covenant-relationship of the people of Israel with their God. Similarly, the *Bar Mitzvah* ceremony is not an initiatory rite, as such; it developed late as a ceremonial ritual. In Biblical times, the age of maturity and civic responsibility was set at twenty, when the individual could bear arms. As the Jewish national state began to decay during the Roman occupation of Palestine, even greater emphasis was placed upon the work of the religious schools as the principal means of keeping the Jewish nation alive. There had always been a tradition of an educated laity, as we have seen. This tradition was strengthened now that the power of the priests was waning and political sovereignty was slowly being transferred from Jewish hands to those of their Latin conquerors. Telescoping the history of this tradition in a few terse sentences, and bringing it down to their times, the rabbis of the Talmud explain:

In the ancient days (Biblical period) every father taught his own son. The fatherless boy (and it should be added, the child of an ignorant father) was given no instruction. Later schools were erected in Jerusalem, where the boys were sent from all over the country. But these were inadequate. The fatherless were still left without teaching. Thereupon schools were opened in the largest town of every district to which youths of sixteen or seventeen, who could do without the care of their parents, were sent. But it was soon apparent that school discipline had no effect upon young men who had come in as adolescents. Then, finally, schools were instituted in every city and town for children of six or seven.

(Talmud: Baba Batra 21a.)

So deeply had their reverent attitude toward learning become ingrained in the Jewish psyche that prospective bridegrooms were counseled to make education the touchstone for their choice of mates. The rabbis recommended that:

One should always sell everything one possesses in order to marry the daughter of a scholar: if he does not find a scholar's daughter, he should marry the daughter of the great men of the generation; if he does not find a daughter of great men, he should marry the daughter of archisynagogi; if he does not find a daughter of archisynagogi, he should marry the daughter of charity supervisors, he should marry the daughter of elementary teachers, *but he should never marry the daughter of the illiterate people of the land.*

(Talmud: Pesahim 49b.)

Thus it is not unusual to find the Rabbis of this period prescribing a ladder of education—a ladder which is ultimately responsible for the development of *Bar Mitzvah* as a symbolic, educational ceremony signifying religious readiness on the part of the adolescent male. They taught: "At five years, the age is reached for the study of Scripture; at ten, for the study of the Mishnah; at thirteen, for the fulfillment of the commandments; at fifteen, for the study of the Talmud . . ." Since, at the age of thirteen, a young man had

[73]

already engaged in the study of the Hebrew Bible as well as the rabbinical interpretations codified in the Mishnah, he was deemed ready and fit to undertake the obligations of the Law, as a responsible member of the Jewish community in his own right.

Since a Jewish boy reaches religious majority at the age of thirteen—for by then, he is expected to be literate in the Law —thereafter he may be counted as one of the *minyan,* the quorum of ten males required for the conduct of public services. Yet the *Bar Mitzvah* ceremony is only a symbol of his new privilege, and even if a boy should not have performed these rites, if he is over thirteen, he is counted as a member of the congregation. Like all other Jewish rituals, *Bar Mitzvah* is not like a Christian sacrament, in which an inward, invisible change has taken place. It is a sign, a remembrance, and a symbol—but most of all, *Bar Mitzvah* is a status in Jewish life, and not merely a ceremonial. In the Jewish view, the change does not take place within the person, as such; rather it marks the age when a change occurs in his obligations vis-à-vis the commandments. Judaism insists that the actual performance of the deed, whether ritual or moral, in conformity with God's law is the essential thing—and the practice of the Law is based upon the fundamental requirement that the Law be studied and understood. In a word: Faith alone will not do; only good works, studied and comprehended, can give content and meaning to a man's faith.

Another of the privileges granted to a boy who has passed his thirteenth birthday, and of which the *Bar Mitzvah* ceremony is a symbol and reminder, is the right to don the *tephillin,* or phylacteries, during morning weekday prayers, at home or in the synagogue. This custom is based upon the Biblical Commandment: "And you shall bind them for a sign upon your hand and they shall be frontlets between your eyes." The phylacteries, like the *tallit,* were also part of the daily dress of Jews in ancient times, and later were adopted for ritual purposes, as a constant reminder of the commandments of God. The phylacteries consist of two small square boxes each with a long leather strap attached to it. One is worn on the head, the other on the biceps of the left arm, pointing to the heart—symbolic reminders that Jews must follow God's laws with all their hearts and minds.

In the head phylactery there are four strips of parchment, each in a separate compartment. Each contains Biblical passages, written in Hebrew, which deal with some of the essentials of the faith: the liberation from the bondage of Egypt as a reminder of God, the Redeemer, and the basic "creed" of Judaism— "Hear, O, Israel the Lord, Our God, the Lord is One." In the phylactery of the arm these same passages are written on one piece of parchment. The Hebrew letter *shin* is stamped on the box of the head phylactery, the letter *yod* on the arm phylactery, and the strap of the head-piece is tied in the back into a knot shaped like the letter *dalet*. In Hebrew, these letters spell *shaddai*—Almighty—a suggestion that by wearing the *tephillin* each morning, the Jew is reminded of his duty to God. Indeed, the *tephillin* should be donned for prayer before one is permitted to eat: man's first responsibility each morning is to give thanks to God for the gift of life, and only then may he think of his own physical needs. Because the Sabbath and holy days are themselves day-long reminders of this duty, the *tephillin* are worn for prayer only on weekdays (Sundays, as well), but not on these other occasions.

We have been describing the way in which young Jewish men are inducted into their religious obligations, and no doubt the reader has been wondering why young women seem to have little or no share in these procedures. Actually, the early rabbis who helped to mold these patterns were keenly aware of the fact that women play an important part in the religious life. It was their belief, however, that certain of the commandments were given to the men, others to the women. In practice, they developed an approach to the ritual in which the synagogue service, like that of the earlier

Temple service, was conducted by men, while the religious life of the home was largely placed in the hands of the wife and mother. We will have occasion to see how this has helped to strengthen the life of the home throughout the ages. Nevertheless, in recent decades in America, there has developed a public ritual for girls in their twelfth or thirteenth year, known as *Bat Mitzvah,* or daughter of the commandment. In many Conservative and Reform congregations, where this ritual ceremony has been introduced, it has stimulated the interest of young girls in continuing their religious education. Now, they too come before the congregation and read a section of the Scripture, as a sign of their mastery of it and their allegiance to its principles.

A ceremony known as Confirmation is also held in most Reform and Conservative congregations, and even in certain Orthodox synagogues. Generally, it is held on or near the Feast of Weeks, *Shavuot,* which commemorates the giving of the Law on Sinai. It is essentially a graduation exercise, signaling the completion of nine or ten years of elementary religious training, which culminates at age fifteen or sixteen. Here, too, as with *Bar Mitzvah* and *Bat Mitzvah,* the essential hallmark of the ritual for Jewish teen-agers is intimately connected with the process of learning: the Torah and its law are the essential thing. All hope for the continuance of the Jewish way of life is pinned upon it. To paraphrase Scripture, Judaism recognizes that "where there is no learning the people perish."

Thus, great stress is placed by all Jewish congregations upon the need for young people to continue their religious education long after the *Bar Mitzvah* and the Confirmation ceremony. Such educational programs require special effort on the part of teen-agers, who are already burdened with the full program of general studies in their public secondary schools. Yet, more and more of them are voluntarily taking Jewish religious courses, supplementary to their regular program of secular studies. In some congregations, provision is even made for special classes and seminars for young people of college age. Indeed, "adult education" is an area of religious programming into which many congregations are presently venturing, and with good results. In addition to courses in the Hebrew language and prayer book, adults attend lecture and study groups which reappraise Bible and religious ideology on a more mature level than is possible in the childhood years.

Not in vain did the rabbis of old teach: "The study of the Law outweighs in importance all of the other commandments . . . for the illiterate man cannot be a pious man . . ."

# VIII Marriage ...

It can be assumed with confidence that long before men had organized public movements and places of religious worship, their spiritual practices were part of the home life. The family was—and for some people still is—the center of devotion, and parents acted as priests of the altar of the hearth. The major object of marriage was to preserve the ideals of the group through the life of the family. This is one of the basic reasons why all organized religious groups are vitally interested in marriage, not only as a ceremony, but as the firm foundation for everything they consider to be sacred. The marriage vows are a symbol of the joint commitment of a man and his wife to a way of life that is holy.

For Jews, in particular, the home is a most essential part of their religious practice. Despite the fact that many synagogue buildings were razed during the intolerant Middle Ages, Judaism remained alive, because the stage for so many of its sacred acts was in the home and not the synagogue building. For this reason, the Jewish ban on intermarriage is most strict. It is assumed that a "house divided cannot stand." And this is particularly true of a house like that of the Jews, where religion is so integral a part of daily living. Non-Jews may, of course, convert to Judaism prior to the wedding ceremony. Reform rabbis require only a period of instruction for the convert, after which they will accept him as a full-fledged member of the Jewish people. Orthodox and Conservative rabbis require, in addition, the aforementioned traditional and historical rites: immersion in a pool of running water (a *mikvah*), for the woman convert, and circumcision plus immersion, for a man. In addition (perhaps originally because of the fear of possible physical dangers), there are forty-two kinds of relatives which Jews may not marry, including step-mothers, step-fathers, aunts and nieces. Other religious and civil groups have similarly banned what are called incestuous or consanguineous marriages.

Before we discuss the religious life of the Jewish family, it is well that we learn something about the nature of Jewish marriage and examine the wedding ceremony itself. In Judaism, man's highest station is achieved through married life. Judaism begins with the basic conviction that since man is a creation of God, no element of his nature in inherently evil or sinful. That is why it frowns upon celibacy and has never regarded marriage as a concession to the weakness of human flesh. On the contrary, marriage is considered to be a sacred duty, a fundamental *mitzvah*. The rabbis taught, with characteristic psychological insight: "He who reaches the age of twenty and does not marry, spends all his days in sin—or, at least in the thought of sin."

Early Christianity was of a different opinion, largely as a result of the influence of Paul's teachings. He was trained in Greek thought and accepted the idea of a division between body and soul. The Greeks believed that the physical aspects of life were the source of all evil, while the spiritual components were productive of goodness and purity. Paul apparently believed in this eternal dichotomy between body and soul. The body, with its physical desires, was lustful and sinful; the soul was the seat of the highest spiritual longings of man. Thus, it followed that the body's cravings had to be suppressed in order to achieve the highest in life: celibacy, for Paul, was the supreme personal goal. However, since most people could not be expected to conquer their physical impulses, the institution of marriage was established in Christianity as a concession to the baser elements in human nature. But since it was permitted as a concession, escape from it, in the form of divorce, was not to be made easy or, for that matter, at all possible.

Because it never recognized that Greek dualism—the antagonism between body and soul—as a true picture of human nature, Judaism continued to insist upon the essential unity of man's nature. The body was not evil in itself, nor was it the source of evil. Man worships God with his body, as well as with his soul, the rabbis taught. The first *mitzvah* in the Mosaic Law, they pointed out, was the commandment to "be fruitful and multiply" (Gen. 1:28).

For these same reasons, Judaism came to regard divorce, not as a punishment for a crime, but as a frank recognition that the marriage was not fulfilling its sacred purposes. Just as marriage is integrally a part of the religious life, so is its dissolution; thus, in addition to the solemnizing of the wedding in accordance with Jewish ritual practice, Orthodox and Conservative rabbis also require that a religious bill of divorce, called a *get,* be issued by a rabbinical court once the civil decree is granted. The Reform Jewish practice in this matter parallels closely the contention of some of the early Protestant reformers that the laws of marriage and divorce and their regulation are purely secular affairs, to be regulated by the state. To be sure, there was some disagreement on the question of divorce among the early rabbis. The school of Shammai ruled that divorce was prohibited except when adultery had been committed. The other school, that of gentle Hillel, whose views prevailed, permitted divorce on other grounds as well. The New Testament apparently adopted the view of Shammai, undoubtedly because such a view fitted in more closely with its understanding of human nature. The Jewish conception of man is quite different from that of the Christians, and its viewpoint is reflected not only in theological matters but concretely in such matters as marriage and divorce.

Because the home is so central in Judaism, it is actually symbolized at the Jewish wedding service itself. The ceremony may take place anywhere, and any learned Jew may perform it, although it has become the practice to restrict this right to rabbis and cantors. But always, in a traditional ceremony, there is the marriage canopy, called a *huppah,* under which the participants stand. The canopy is the symbol of the home which this marriage is about to establish. As part of the ritual, the rabbi offers to the bride and the groom two cups of wine, the symbol of life's goodness. Wine will later be used in their home at virtually all religious occasions; it represents the gifts of God's bounties and their joy in sharing them. The ring is symbolical of the consummation of the marriage and of its sanctity. As the groom places it upon the bride's finger, he announces the meaning of the whole ceremony with these words: "Behold, you are *consecrated* unto me, with this ring, according to the laws of Moses and the people of Israel." He places the ring upon the forefinger of his bride's right hand. This is a Semitic custom which was established so that all could easily see that this woman was married and not available to other men. The right hand was probably chosen for its dexterity and the forefinger because of its prominence. The bride wears a veil, a custom that also comes out of the same early background; for, among Semitic peoples, unmarried girls never appeared unveiled in public. Only at the very end of the ceremony does she lift the veil, to indicate that she is now a married woman.

The various provisions for the man's maintenance of his wife and the mutual obligations both have toward each other are detailed in the marriage contract, called the *ketubah*. These include both the physical and spiritual needs of the man and his bride. Before the ceremony begins, this contract is witnessed by two men, neither of whom may be related to the bride or the groom—the officiating rabbi, if not a relation, may act as one of these witnesses. The text of the *ketubah* was composed during the period when the vernacular of the Jews in Palestine was Aramaic, and it is still printed in that language as a link to the past. After the rabbi reads the marriage contract in the original and in English translation, he, or the cantor, recite what are called the "Seven Benedictions." These are devoted to an expression of thanks to God for the institution of marriage and the family; for having implanted His image on the human race; and for the joy of the wedding and the happiness of the bride and the groom. One of these benedictions, in addition, offers a prayer for the restoration of Jerusalem. Ancient Jewish sentiment, based on Psalm 137, reminds the Jew to recall Jerusalem "above your chiefest joy." And that is why such a prayer is included at such a supremely happy moment as the wedding service. For the same reason, the traditional ceremony concludes with the groom breaking a glass under his heel, to commemorate the destruction of Jerusalem. A Reform Jewish wedding ceremony will differ in a number of details. The canopy and the *ketubah* are generally omitted, as is the special prayer for the restoration of Jerusalem. Most of the service is in English, and invariably it is rendered by a rabbi. For all Jews, however, marriage is a sacred act, and for that reason it is called *kiddushin,* or sanctification.

Like Jews, most other religious groups have strong feelings against intermarriage. It represents a grave risk of religious infidelity and, for the children of such a marriage, the serious possibility of being spiritual hybrids, rooted in no concrete religious tradition.

In earliest times, marriage was virtually a commercial act, necessary to the tribal economy, and woman was considered as a mere chattel. In Judaism and Christianity it has been elevated to an act of mutual consecration, which is related to the spiritual order of life. Indeed, if marriage is not sacred, then nothing else in life can ever be.

# IX ...And the Family

The purpose of marriage is the family and it is in the home that religion is lived each day. Now that we have learned what Judaism means by marriage we are ready to observe how it weaves religious practices into the very texture of home life. To be spiritually fit one needs "spiritual exercise." Faith and hope, like charity, are first learned in the home or they are learned nowhere.

Within a home where the Jewish religion is practiced you are sure to find a number of ritual objects which help establish the mood of reverence. None of these, you will discover, is a holy object in itself which confers sanctity or is worthy of veneration. Since Judaism is not a sacramental religion it has no sacramentals. These ritual objects are there because they will be used as part of the various devotions that go into the making of the religious practices of the Jewish home. There is but one exception to this generalization. As you enter a Jewish home (or a public Jewish building), you will observe a small metal or wood object fastened to the right hand doorpost. This is a *mezzuzah,* within which is a parchment scroll containing, in Hebrew, the "Hear, O Israel . . ." and the Biblical verses which follow it. Through a little opening, the word *shaddai* (Almighty) is visible, the same Hebrew word mentioned in our discussion of the phylacteries. The *mezzuzah* is a denominating symbol, marking out the dwelling as a Jewish home, and reminding its occupants of the ideals and religious practices for which it should stand. The Bible commands: "You shall love the Lord your God, with all your heart, with all your soul, and with all your might." And it goes on to remind the Jew:

> And these words which I command you this day, shall be upon your heart; and you shall teach them diligently unto your children and shall talk of them when you sit in your house, and when you walk by the way, and when you lie down and when you rise up. And you shall bind them for a sign upon your hand, and they shall be for frontlets between your eyes. *And you shall write them upon the doorposts of your house and upon your gates.*

The *mezzuzah,* then, is not a sacred object, and it is assigned no specific function in the performance of any ritual act. Its supreme purpose is just this: To remind the members of the family to fulfill all of their religious obligations both inside and outside of the home. And since these obligations are intended to bring the family to a closer intimacy with God, the *mezzuzah* has the Hebrew word *shaddai,* or "Almighty," placed upon it, as a constant reminder of this thought. Notice, however, that the reminder itself is in the form of a *word* and does not consist of a picture or a graven image.

Inside the home will be found the Sabbath candelabrum, which is kindled by the mother on Friday evenings at dusk. The Sabbath is greeted in the home amid blessings, pronounced over light, which are spoken by the mother. It is the woman who ushers in the spirit of peace and rest. When the Sabbath is over, light again is the symbol of its departure. A special braided candle, large enough to last a year or longer, is used for the home service of *havdalah,* or separation, said on Saturdays at nightfall. Sweet-smelling spices are also used as part of this ritual, as a symbol of the hope that the week about to begin may be a fragrant one. A special ritual spicebox is used for this ceremony. For the bread, over which the praise of God is recited by each person before the meal is begun, specially embroidered cloth covers are used. And for the wine, over which thanks are offered at both the Sabbath welcoming and departure services, as well as on other holidays, fine silver goblets are usually provided. The Sabbath is essentially a family affair, and it is celebrated by parents and children through these rituals.

In the Jewish home, the Bible, and particularly the Pentateuch, is more than just another book on the library shelf. On Friday evenings, it is traditional for the whole family to read the thirty-first chapter of the Book of Proverbs at the dinner table: "A woman of valor who can find? For her price is far above rubies." This is the way in which husband

and children offer their praises to the matriarch of each household for the spirit of the Sabbath which she has helped to create, and for the manifold ministries which are hers. After dinner, in traditional homes, it is the custom to read aloud and to comment upon the weekly Scripture lesson, the *sidrah,* which is to be read at the synagogue service on the morrow. The practice of reading the Bible aloud at home following Sunday services has found its way into Christian homes via the Jewish home. For in the traditional Jewish home, the Bible is a well-studied book.

The Jewish home also counts among its proud possessions other ritual objects which it uses on the sacred days of the religious year. There is the *Hanukkah Menorah,* the nine-branched candelabrum, used during the Feast of Lights in winter. And in many Jewish homes one will find an ornamental box for the *etrog,* or citron, which plays a prominent part in the ritual for the fall holiday of *Sukkot,* the Feast of Tabernacles. On this holiday, some families still erect a small booth in their backyard, adorning it with fruits and flowers of the season. They will take most of their meals inside the *Sukkah* for the duration of the holiday, in remembrance of the Biblical injunction: "You shall dwell in booths seven days . . ." (Lev. 23:42).

For Passover, celebrated in the spring, a whole group of special items are kept. There is the *seder* plate, which contains the ritual foods symbolical of the Passover Exodus. The *seder,* or "Order of Service," is a home service, presided over by the father and attended by many relatives and guests. At the table, the drama of the liberation from Egypt is re-enacted through Biblical readings and ritual symbols. Only unleavened bread, or *matzah,* is eaten for the entire eight days which are celebrated by the Orthodox and Conservatives, or for the seven days observed by Reform Jews. Moreover, the rules of diet for Passover prohibit the eating of anything that has been prepared or has come in contact with any kind of leavening. All of this is done to remind the Jew of the difficulties suffered by his ancestors in Egypt until God made Himself known to them and redeemed them "with a mighty hand and an outstretched arm." The remembrance of what God did for them in Egypt—God as their liberator and redeemer—runs through all of the Jewish religious calendar, as we shall see later.

But what has diet to do with religion, one may ask? Observant Jews believe that it has a great deal to do with the spiritual life, as they understand it! While some may question this relationship between dietary practice and religion, closer examination of many other religions will reveal that special food habits are not restricted to Jews alone. "Man doth not live by bread alone," and he translates this idea into dramatic personal practices, through various self-disciplines. Fasting, for example, has entered Christianity via Judaism, and the various Christian practices which accompany the forty days of Lent, while not derived directly from Judaism, do reflect the Hebraic concepts which place food into the orbit of religious living. Catholics observe days of "complete abstinence," on Fridays, Ash Wednesday, and Holy Saturday, when meat and soup or gravy made from meat may not be eaten. They must also fast before they receive Holy Communion, unless they have received special dispensation. Until about a thousand years ago, it was necessary for Christians to avoid eating blood or blood-filled meat. To this day, Moslems do not eat the flesh of swine. And Buddhists, too, follow regulations which were adopted about the seventh century, forbidding the use of all meats. Thus, food habits, as part of religious living, are not restricted to Jews alone.

But what are the special meanings which the Jewish dietary laws, the *kosher* laws, seek to convey? The answer to this question supplies a necessary insight into the value system of Judaism. But, before answering, a brief word is in order regarding the rules themselves.

There are no restrictions on vegetables and fruits, but

among living creatures many species are forbidden. All winged insects and creeping things, which multiply quickly and are a pest to man, are prohibited. For fish to be fit, or *kosher,* they must have fins and scales; oysters, lobsters, and other shell-fish are thus prohibited. Among the mammals, only those which have cloven hoofs and chew the cud are permitted; thus, virtually all wild animals are excluded. As for fowl, the Bible specifically lists the forbidden varieties among which are vultures, hawks, owls, pelicans, ravens, and storks.

The dietary rules also extend to the manner in which all warm-blooded animals are prepared for food. The slaughtering knife must be sharp, so as not to cause the animal any unnecessary pain. The animal must not be stunned before slaughtering, for this would prevent the free flow of blood, and the absorption of the blood into the meat makes the food prohibited. Only one expert in slaughtering who is observant of the laws of Jewish piety may perform this ritual act. He is a functionary of the Jewish community known as a *shohet,* and he must receive authorization from a rabbi. After slaughtering, the animal is examined in order to ascertain that there are no symptoms of communicable diseases, any of which would render it unfit for food. When the housewife prepares the meat for her home table, she salts it in order to let out as much blood as possible. Or, if the meat is to be broiled, the fire itself acts as the agent for the removal of blood.

There is still another dietary rule of significance. Three times Scripture records a rule against seething a kid in its mother's milk. According to Maimonides, a great medieval rabbi and physician, this regulation was originally intended to extirpate an idolatrous practice, common among Israel's neighbors. It was later interpreted as prohibiting the cooking or eating of the meat of any warm-blooded animal with milk or its derivative. That is why observant Jews do not eat meat with milk, butter, or cheese at the same meal. In addition, in order to avoid any possibility of mixing meat with milk, traditional Jewish homes use two sets of dishes, one of which is used only for meat foods, the other only for milk foods.

With this background, we now return to our former question: How do Jews understand these rules to be a contribution to their spiritual life? In Christianity, and particularly in its Catholic form, the table has become the church altar in a new and mysterious way. When Holy Communion is taken, food takes on a supernatural, symbolical meaning. For the Jews, food is never a symbol of the supernatural. The laws of diet are intended to make the table an altar, not by a mysterious transition, but rather by making the daily acts of eating into sacred and sanctifying moments. If a creature's life must be taken in order to sustain human life, then, at least, let the physical act of eating be a religious act and not merely a carnivorous, cannibal-like performance. For such reasons, every meal is hallowed by moments of prayer, before and after one eats, and traditional-minded Jews will cover their heads for prayer at the dinner table, just as they do when they pray in the synagogue or at home. Indeed, every time a pious Jew places food in his mouth, he will recite an appropriate benediction of divine thanks; there are special blessings for bread, vegetables, fruit, wine, and even for water. Food, then, to the religious Jew, is a sign and a reminder of man's dependence on God, and his gratitude to the Almighty for the bounty of life.

Regarding the special rules prohibiting certain kinds of food, it would be useless to speculate on the possible hygienic reasons for every one of their details, although many have tried to do so. Many of these regulations are undoubtedly the result of ancient practices and mores, the exact reasons for which are not known to us. What is significant, however, is that they have been invested with religious meaning by being transformed into moral and educational acts. It should be pointed out that none of the animals considered fit for Jewish food is carnivorous. There is a moral meaning to this: Carnivorous animals thrive on their acts of murder.

What is prohibited here is the enjoyment of food obtained through the continual destruction of living creatures. While one is permitted to kill for food, it is only a necessary evil, and the act of killing must be conducted in a way that will engender a religious mood. The *shohet,* or ritual slaughterer, must be mindful of the non-righteous aspects of his work, and he therefore must kill the animal with the least amount of pain. Hunting animals for sport, and not for sustenance, is strictly prohibited by the Jewish tradition, in order to train men to resist any act which would turn them into parasites. Blood is considered to be the symbol of the life-force, "for the life of the flesh is in the blood" (Lev. 17:11). For this reason, every care is taken to extract as much blood as possible, in the slaughtering, and in the preparation of the animal for use as food at the table. Even eggs which have blood spots in them may not be eaten.

While some Jews, particularly those of the Reform group, no longer observe all of the dietary rules, these regulations have played an extremely important part in molding the life of the Jewish family. Through them, the mother of each household has been given a special religious role in the conduct of religious life. Every time she prepares a meal, she is mindful that she is engaging in a Jewish religious act, and not merely feeding her family. Through her ministry, she helps develop a way of life in her home which her children perceive from their childhood on.

An ongoing series of religious activities permeates the entire household, and early in life these help the young Jew to establish a sense of loyalty to the Jewish faith. If, in the past. Jewish families defied many of the sociological trends of disorganization, it was the various home rituals which helped to constitute the "secret weapon" of the Jewish religious community.

# x Death

To the religious person death comes as part of the natural plan of life. It is inevitable, as everyone realizes. But to the truly devout, death is something to prepare for throughout life. To every religious man, death is not the end of life.

For these reasons, Jews, as well as other religious groups, face death with the assurances and the comfort afforded by the rites of their faith. Here again, as before, by observing what these rites are, we learn much about the beliefs they symbolize.

According to Jewish tradition, when a person is about to die he recites the *viddui,* or confession, a rite connected with the belief in life after death. In his last conscious moments he addresses these words to God:

> May it be Your will to heal me completely. Yet, if it is deter-
> mined that I die, I will accept it at your hand with love. Father
> of the fatherless and Judge of the widow protect my beloved
> ones...

His final words are those which stand at the center of all Jewish belief. "Hear, O Israel, the Lord is our God, the Lord is one"—the unshakeable affirmation of the unity of God and the world He has created.

Once death has come, the body is washed and dressed in linen shrouds. At one time in Jewish history, the wealthy were buried in costly garments. But Rabban Gamaliel II, a distinguished rabbi and scholar who lived at the beginning of the second century C.E., asked that he be interred in a shroud similar to those used by the poor. Since that time, this custom has been adopted by traditional Jews, to stress the equality of all men. As a further demonstration of this idea, Jews are buried in the simplest of coffins; expensive metal caskets are at variance with traditional Jewish proce-dure.

Some congregations permit the use of their own chapels for the funeral services of their own members. Usually, the funeral service is conducted in the synagogue only in the ase of people who have made significant contributions to he religious life of the group. In earlier times, these services vere held only in the home of the deceased and, in our day, hey are most often conducted there, and in special establishments known as funeral chapels. A rabbi usually leads he ritual, although there is no rigid order of service. Selections from appropriate psalms are usually chosen, and an address of eulogy ordinarily follows. The service closes with a prayer for the repose of the soul of the deceased, which may also be repeated at the graveside. At the time of burial the mourners recite a prayer of doxology, known as the *Kaddish*. This is the prayer which children will recite thrice daily at a synagogue service for eleven months following the death of their parents. This prayer extols the sovereignty of God in human life; it never mentions death. It is intended as a grand affirmation of God's majesty and beneficence in human life. Thus, the Jew is taught to thank God for the gift of life when physical life comes to an end. In Job's words: "The Lord hath given; the Lord hath taken. . . . Praised be the name of the Lord."

Before the burial, close relatives make a slight tear in their clothes as a visible sign of mourning. This custom, known as *keriah,* or tearing, is based upon the Biblical precedent of publicly rending one's garments at a time of death. The tear is made as the mourners stand erect, and they recite a blessing signifying their resolute resignation to God's justice: "Blessed are You, O Lord, our God, King of the universe, the true Judge."

Immediately following the funeral, the family returns home to begin a whole week of private mourning. This period is known as *shivah,* or the "seven days" signifying the full week of mourning. During the week, the mourners do not engage in any gainful occupation, and they do not leave their homes, even for public prayers, except on the Sabbath. Instead, prayer services are conducted in the home, and often friends who have come to console the family will also participate. To be sure, if one's livelihood is at stake, he may return to work, even during the seven-day period. In addition, if it is impossible to gather the necessary ten men required for group worship, the mourners may leave their homes to attend the daily morning and evening services in the synagogue. The week is to be spent in quiet meditation, and a memorial lamp burns throughout this period. Often, the mourners will read such books as Job or Lamentations as spiritual aids in contemplating the significance of the tragedy that has come upon them. Mirrors, considered a sign of luxury, are covered over for the week's intense mourning.

Parents, sons and daughters, brothers and sisters, husbands or wives—only these close relatives are required to sit at home for the period of a week. After the week is concluded, they continue to show respect for the dead by not engaging in public forms of entertainment for another three weeks. In all, a full month, or thirty days of mourning in this manner, are required. Observant Jews follow this pattern of mourning for a whole year following the death of a parent, and on every anniversary of the parent's death, the family observes a solemn day of memorial, known as *Yahrzeit*. This is a German word, because the custom assumed its present form among German Jews. On that day, the male children make it a point to attend synagogue services, and at the conclusion of the prayers, they recite the *Kaddish*. A memorial lamp, similar to the one used during *shivah*, is kindled from sunset to sunset during the twenty-four hour period of this annual observance. In addition, public memorial services for the dead, known as *Yizkor* (remembrance) services, are conducted in the synagogue four times during the year, on the Day of Atonement and the three harvest festivals. Sometimes, before the end of the first year after death, a tombstone is erected over the grave. In addition to the usual inscription, it often carries the Hebrew names of the deceased and of his father. This is customary Jewish nomenclature, and can e traced back to Biblical times. Thus Moses was known as Moses, the son of Amram.

The Jewish strategy of solace, if one may call it such, is intended to bring the mourner back into the community after a short period of withdrawal, so that he may find comfort through identification with the ideals of the group. From the moment his beloved is interred, the Jew is bound by strong ties to the synagogue and the congregation. When one of his parents dies, he will attend religious services at the synagogue for virtually a whole year, and during this time will come to see the needs of the community, as well as the sorrow of others like himself. Moreover, Judaism has arranged a kind of hierarchical order in the process of mourning, with well-arranged time steps. The first seven days after the burial are the days of most intense mourning, and there is much privacy during this period. But there is a gradual tapering off of that intensity of grief in the following thirty days, and in the next ten months. These are the days when personal grief is transcended through the synagogue, and the mourner learns the meaning of sorrow through spiritual service. Through his religious practices, as the days become weeks and the weeks months, the Jewish mourner may come to know the deepest meaning of Job's words: "The Lord has given and the Lord has taken away. Praised be the name of the Lord." The wisdom of knowing how to face life and death may come slowly, but it comes to many who learn to submerge their sorrows in the life of the group.

Catholics and Protestants have borrowed several Jewish customs for use in their funeral procedures. At the conclusion of the Mass preceding Catholic burials, the priest puts on a black cape and turns to the place where the body lies. The service that follows is known as the Absolution. He sprinkles the coffin with holy water to symbolize the preservation of the body and soul from the power of Satan. Then he takes the censer, in which incense is burning, and incenses the coffin on all sides. Incense is used

by the Church primarily during the solemn Masses and
this use harks back to the practice of the Jewish priest
when they performed their worship in the ancient Temple
But since the destruction of the Temple, spices are used
in Jewish religious rites only for the ceremony of *havdalah*
when the Sabbath is over, as a symbol of the hope for
a sweet and fragrant week to come. In the Church, how
ever, incense has been given a mystical meaning: its burning
symbolizes the zeal of faith; its fragrance, Christian virtue
its rising smoke, the ascent of prayer before the throne of
God. Like the Jews, Catholics also annually commemorate
the anniversaries of their beloved dead. On that day they
attend a special solemn Mass. Thus, through faith, the life
of each generation is linked to the other, and death is not the
end but the beginning of remembrance.

Protestant liturgical services for the dead, like those of the
Catholics, generally make use of a number of appropriate
Psalms from the Hebrew Bible, the 23rd and 90th Psalms
being the most widely used. In at least two fundamental
respects, Protestants view the church's role in helping the
Christian face death in much the same way as do the Jews
They feel that one of the purposes of the church at the time
of death is to relate people to God in such a way that they
may draw upon the resources of His spirit in their hour of
confusion and grief. This attitude has always been held by
the Jews: *Kaddish,* which the Jewish mourner recites, em
phasizes the sovereignty of God, and its purpose is to bring
man comfort through the faith that even though God has
brought to pass an alteration in life, He will provide the
strength which is needed to stand up to it.

Still another purpose of the church at the time of death
touches on the aspect of Christian fellowship—the com
munity of believers who make up the church. Through the
church, the individual senses that his grief is being shared
for there the joys of one are the joys of all and the sorrows of
one the sorrows of all. This idea has come into Christianity as

a consequence of Jewish practices of mourning. The week of Jewish home devotions, when neighbors come to offer consolation, and the daily devotions at the synagogue in the presence of the congregation, among whom are other mourners, similarly afflicted—these are the means which Judaism uses to support its people when death comes.

# PART III SACRED TIMES AND SEASONS

# xi The Calendar and Doctrine

The laws of nature help man to sharpen his understanding of time. Primitive men had little sense of history, and so their calendars reflected only the changing rhythm of the seasons. But early in Jewish thought we are confronted with a different and revolutionary idea. The Jews were not only interested in nature but also in history. They believed in God's sovereignty over the world of nature. But because they believed that God had created man, as well as the world, they were conscious of His guiding presence in the events that make up the life of men and nations.

Their festivals were, at first, celebrations linked to the natural order, and the dates were established by the life in nature. The Jewish month began with the new moon, and the dates of all festivals were determined by the phases of the moon. Thus, for example, Passover and the Feast of Booths coincide with the first full moon of spring and autumn, respectively. But to express their special interest in things that went beyond nature into history, they celebrated a holiday each week which was not determined by the natural order. This was their weekly Sabbath, given to man to teach him to reflect upon the meaning of human life. At first the Sabbath was linked primarily to the significance of creation for human life. But it came to be a weekly reminder of the power of God to enter human history as the force that redeems. The Ten Commandments teach this most significant interpretation of the Sabbath day. The first time they are recorded, in the Book of Exodus, they explain the meaning of the Sabbath as a weekly memorial of creation, "for in six days the Lord made heaven and earth, the sea, and all that is in them, and rested on the seventh day; wherefore the Lord blessed the Sabbath day and hallowed it." But with the passage of years, this new meaning was added, as given in the Book of Deuteronomy, where the commandments are recorded for a second time: "And you shall remember that you were a servant in the land of Egypt, and the Lord your God brought you out thence by a mighty hand and an outstretched arm; therefore the Lord your God commanded you to keep the Sabbath day."

For this reason, the festivals also came to have new meaning. They were no longer only a record of the passing of the seasons, as they once had been. They were made to commemorate God's activity in history, as the redeemer and liberator. The history of the Jews might have been insignificant, if they were just another nation. But they considered themselves chosen by God to teach the world the meaning of His oneness. Therefore, they believed that what happened to them was important to everybody, because it was a demonstration of God's work in the world, through the people of Israel. Their history became sacred; indeed, it became the very basis of their theology. Thus, the sacred calendar of the Jewish people is essentially a re-enactment of the historical events in the life of Israel. Jewish celebrations of religious holidays are interpretations of the idea of God as the redeemer in the living events of history.

Despite the fact that the Sabbath occurs with weekly regularity, it is, with the exception of the Day of Atonement, the most significant of all Jewish religious commemorations. Indeed, in order to describe the special significance of the Day of Atonement as the most solemn of Jewish religious holy days, Scripture borrows the word "Sabbath" in order to highlight the extreme importance of that day and calls it the "Sabbath of Sabbaths." Virtually all the themes which are emphasized in the other major festivals find some echo in the Sabbath itself.

The essential significance of the Sabbath day is summed up in a single word—holiness. In Jewish Scripture the people of Israel are commanded over and over again: "You shall be holy!" And for this reason they are instructed to separate themselves from certain things, places, or foods which symbolize the profane aspects of human life. Holiness requires acts of separation; we must stand aside from the ordinary in order to achieve the extraordinary. The Sabbath is a holy day whose regimen of conduct is designed to set the Jews apart from mundane affairs, to sanctify a part of the week in order that the whole of the week may reflect a consecrated approach to life.

The Sabbath day, like all other days of the week in the Jewish religion, begins at sundown the evening before. It is symbolically made to serve sacred purposes alone with the recitation of a prayer of consecration at the beginning of the festive meal, on Friday evening. This prayer, known as *kiddush*, sets aside the 24 hours which are to follow for higher thought and spiritual reflection, for prayer, meditation, and learned study. In the *kiddush*, which is recited over a brimful cup of wine, the symbol of bounty, there is reflected more than the concept of Sabbath peace alone; references are made to the liberation from the bondage of Egypt, as well as to the joys which come from the spirit of restfulness which descend upon the foregathered family.

Observant Jews do not perform any significant labors on the Sabbath day. In the morning they attend synagogue services, returning home for a festive noon luncheon which is accompanied by songs of praise and table hymns. The afternoon is often the time when families join in reading from sacred texts, discussing earnest and serious matters of human consequence. Before sunset, the afternoon prayers are recited, and they are followed by a "service of separation." It is as if the Jew has been endowed on the Sabbath day with an additional soul—an added measure of spirit and sweetness attends him. He takes his leave of the Sabbath with almost mournful sounds, for he knows that within a few hours he must return to the practical and material world, to the marketplace, the shop, and the office. With the setting of the sun, he participates, either in the synagogue or in the home, in a ceremony known as *havdalah,* or separation, which sets apart the sanctity of the Sabbath from the ordinariness of the day about to begin.

As a sign of their love for the Sabbath and their eager

anticipation of its return, Jews number the days of the week in terms of their proximity to the Sabbath day. Thus, Sunday is known as the first day of the week; there remain six days more for the arrival of the Sabbath—and so with Monday, the second day of the week, and Tuesday the third day of the week, and so on. Finally, when the evening of the sixth day arrives, the eve of the Sabbath, the religious Jew joyfully knows that the labors for the week have come to an end. And like the Almighty, as described in the first pages of the Book of Genesis, he looks upon all of his work during the days preceding as a prelude to a day of recreation. God rested on the seventh day from all the labors of Creation, to teach man that the highest form of recreation is the spiritual rest and profound contemplation of the meaning of Creation.

The days, as well as the months and the seasons, have been given spiritual significance. Yet the present structure of the Jewish calendar has an interesting history, which reflects some of the problems of Jewish doctrine and thought. In Biblical times the Jewish year began with the first month of the spring, the time of planting. The months of the year were twelve in number, and the first day of the month was celebrated as a semi-festival. The period of one new moon to another consists of approximately twenty-nine days and twelve hours, making a total of about 354 days to the lunar year. In addition to the new moon, whose appearance was celebrated as a religious event, the religious commemorations took place during the seasons of the year which were related to the agricultural life of the early Hebrews. This is why, in Biblical times, the new year began with the first month of spring, the time of planting.

Thus, the Jewish calendar was based upon both the lunar as well as the solar year. Since there is a discrepancy of about eleven days between the two, for the sun-based year consists of about 365 days, it became necessary, even in Biblical times, to make up the difference between these two at the end of each year by adding eleven leap days. In this fashion it was possible to preserve the dual needs of the Jewish religious calendar: to retain the religious significance of the new moons, as well as to make certain that Passover would always fall in the springtime and the other harvest festivals would all be commemorated in their proper seasons. For if eleven days were not added at the end of each 354-day lunar year, within a few years Passover would fall in the winter, summer, or fall instead of the spring. But one major problem still remained: The eleven days which were added at the end of each lunar year were not part of the regular calendar, and thus had no name or identity. To overcome this problem, it became necessary to revamp the method of aligning the lunar and solar years. This developed some time in the post-Biblical period and was probably influenced by Meton, the Greek astronomer, who, in the year 432 B.C.E., had reformed the Athenian calendar on the basis of a cycle of 19 years. This cycle consisted of 235 lunar months, the equivalent of the number of days in 19 solar years. He accomplished this by adding a whole month to the lunar year, seven times in the 19 year cycle. Ever since the Jewish calendar was reformed, under the probable influence of Meton, Jews intercalate a whole leap month seven times in 19 years. In this way, the lunar year is brought into line with the solar year. The additional month is always added just before the season of spring in order to make certain that Passover may be celebrated in the springtime of the year. It is known as Adar II (see table on page 108).

There was one further problem which the special religious requirements of Judaism made upon the structure of the calendar. It was necessary to prevent the Day of Atonement— a solemn fast day—from falling either on Friday or on Sunday. This was in consideration of the needs of people who were asked to sanctify the Day of Atonement by rigorous fasting. If this day were to fall on a Friday, it would make it well-nigh impossible for Jews to prepare food in order to break their fast on Friday night, since the Sabbath laws would be in operation at that time, prohibiting the preparation of food. Similarly, if the Day of Atonement were to fall on Sunday, it would mean that food preparations for the ending of the fast would have to take place on Saturday—which, for the very reasons indicated, would also be a violation of the Sabbath. Thus, in order not to make the fast of the Day of Atonement last more than a single 24-hour period, the calendar had to be organized in such a way as to prevent the occurrence of this solemn day on either a Friday or a Sunday. Quite obviously, certain mathematical calculations were required to make this possible by structuring the calendar scientifically. A number of rabbis in the first century of the Christian Era became quite adept in the field of astronomy and mathematics, in order to deal with the many questions involved in fixing the Jewish calendar. They arranged that there be three types of regular years, as well as three types of leap years. The regular year would consist of 353, 354, or 355 days. Normally, the regular lunar year consisted of 354 days, but because of this Friday-Sunday problem, the rabbis established regular years of 353, 354, or 355 days. The Day of Atonement might fall on a Friday or a Sunday if it were always to consist of 354 days. To avoid this, it became necessary to alternate the number of days in the regular lunar year by adding a day or subtracting a day from the regular 354-day period. In a leap year, the same principle was followed. It consisted of 383, 384, 385 days, as one full month is added to the regular lunar period. This was accomplished by permitting three months, Heshvan, Kislev, and Adar to vary in length in regular or leap years—29 or 30 days—in order to accommodate the problem of Atonement.

Since so much of the calendar depends upon the arrival of the new moon, there were at first many problems connected with fixing the exact time of its arrival. By the second century, the procedure of determining the calendar was as follows: On the 30th day of the month the Council of Rabbis (Sanhedrin) met in Jerusalem to hear testimony from witnesses who claimed to have seen the new moon. If the testimony was accepted as being correct, the Council of Rabbis proclaimed the new month as beginning the first day of the new moon. If, however, no witnesses appeared before the Council to make a deposition regarding the new moon, then the new moon was considered as beginning on the day following. The Council of Rabbis proclaimed the new moon by means of fire signals from the hilltops of Judea, thus informing the communities in and around Jerusalem of the official beginning of the new month. Jews who lived at a greater distance and who could not be so informed, observed the 30th day of each month and the day following—two full days—as the new moon, in order to be certain that one of these days, at least, was properly commemorated.

However, as the rabbis became more and more proficient in the science of astronomy, they tended to depend less and less on the testimony of the witnesses. Frequently the first crescent of the new moon was so thin, and it set so soon after the sun, that it was impossible to be certain whether or not it had actually been observed. Ultimately, the rabbis recorded their own astronomical calculations and knew from their scientific observations the exact time of the birth of the new moon. But old traditions die hard. In the distant communities of Babylonia it had already become acceptable for the Jews to observe all the Biblical festivals for an additional day in order to be certain that they would at least observe the proper days to begin with. But in Palestine, which was nearer to the Council of Rabbis, and where, within hours after the official proclamation of the new moon, this information could be known by all, it was unnecessary to add this extra day. The Bible establishes Passover as a seven-day commemoration; in Palestine it was so observed, whereas in the communities outside the holy land it became an eight-day festival. There was a similar method of handling the two other harvest festivals—Shavuot and Sukkot; the former was observed for one day in Palestine and two days in the Diaspora, and the latter for seven days in Palestine and eight days in the communities outside. Once again, however, in order not to impose undue hardship upon the people, the fast Day of Atonement was commemorated both in Palestine and outside of the land for only one day.

Despite the fact that the original reason for adding days to the Biblical requirements of Passover, Shavuot, and Sukkot no longer exists, to this day, all Jews who live outside of the land of Israel, except the Reform group, continue to follow the ancient tradition.

In relation to other calendars, it is of interest to note that the Jewish New Year, Rosh Ha-shanah, falls any time between September 5th to October 4th. The first day of Hanukkah occurs any time from November 27th to December 27th. The first day of Passover may be commemorated any time from March 26th to April 25th.

In the early days of Christianity, a strong and lively rivalry grew up between the Church and Judaism. Some of this is still reflected in the calendars of these groups. Constantine, the first Christian Roman emperor, was described as keeping both the Jewish Sabbath and the Christian Sunday as holy days. Indeed, one of the Church Fathers urged: "Keep holy the Sabbath *and* the Lord's Day, since on the one we commemorate the creation, on the other the resurrection." In the eastern churches, the Jewish Sabbath was kept by Christians for some time. But in the West, where there was a stronger Jewish community, in order to sever the ties to Judaism, the Church converted it into a fast day in preparation for the Sunday worship. Jews, too, reacted in a similar way. Fast days, which were voluntarily undertaken by the ultra-pious, were considered to be quasi-holy days. As part of their legal enactments against Christianity, the rabbis limited the days on which Jews might voluntarily fast to the middle of the week—Mondays and Thursdays. No such fasting was permitted on a Sunday, in order that Christians would not think it was a holy day for Jews. And since Friday was the eve of the Sabbath, a day of joy, it was not permitted to fast then either; moreover, since the early Christians often fasted every Friday in memory of the passion and crucifixion, the rabbis prohibited Jews from fasting on Fridays.

The most well-known example of the way in which the calendar reflected the early Christian-Jewish controversies is the debate which surrounded the fixing of the date of Easter. Until the first Council of Nicaea, in 325 C.E., Christians continued to celebrate Easter at different times. Many of them observed it on the Jewish Passover, the fourteenth day of the Hebrew month of Nissan, which always falls on the first full moon of the spring season. The Council of Nicaea, after great debate and discussion, finally arranged for the fixing of Easter in such a way that it would never fall on this date, but always after it. This is the real meaning behind the final fixing of the Easter date, which has since been established as the authorized practice: Easter is celebrated "on the first Sunday after the full moon on or after the first day of spring, March 21st, or, if the full moon is on Sunday, the next Sunday after."

In Biblical times, as has been indicated, the new year began with the first month of springtime, and the names of the months were called after the seasons of the year. Later, during the Jewish period of exile in Babylonia, the months were given new names, probably of Babylonian origin, and the new year was moved from the spring to the fall of the year. This Babylonian-Jewish nomenclature exists to the present.

On the following page is a table which should be of interest and of help in learning the names of the Jewish months, as well as their relationship to the civil calendar:

| Name of Month | Number | Number of Days | Corresponding to: |
|---|---|---|---|
| **AUTUMN:** | | | |
| Tishri | 1 | 30 | September-October |
| Heshvan | 2 | 29–30 | October-November |
| Kislev | 3 | 29–30 | November-December |
| **WINTER:** | | | |
| Tevet | 4 | 29 | December-January |
| Shevat | 5 | 30 | January-February |
| Adar | 6 | 29–30 | February-March |
| Adar II | | 29 | (Leap year only) |
| **SPRING:** | | | |
| Nissan | 7 | 30 | March-April |
| Iyar | 8 | 29 | April-May |
| Sivan | 9 | 30 | May-June |
| **SUMMER:** | | | |
| Tammuz | 10 | 29 | June-July |
| Av | 11 | 30 | July-August |
| Elul | 12 | 29 | August-September |

# XII The Autumn Holidays

*Rosh Ha-Shanah, The New Year*

The fall's first holiday, *Rosh Ha-Shanah,* or New Year, had to be celebrated for two days, even in Palestine. This was so, because it was the only one of the major festivals to occur on the first day of the month (Tishri), and on the first day of a month there was uncertainty as to the precise time of the new moon in the earlier periods, even in Palestine. Rosh Ha-Shanah is the beginning of a period known as the High Holy Days. It ushers in "Ten Days of Penitence," which conclude with the year's most solemn day—the Day of Atonement. These days, while not "holy days" in themselves, do constitute a time when abstention from worldly pleasures and amusements  helps prod the religious Jew to focus upon his inner life and to take "stock of the state of his soul." For the Jews, the beginning of the year is not a time for hilarity and revelry, but rather a season of spiritual stock-taking devoted to the searching out of one's deeds and misdeeds during the year just concluded. These days are dedicated to God, who is sovereign in the life of men and nations.

In earlier Jewish history several different "new years" were celebrated: The royal new year, for dating the reign of kings; the tithal new year, for reckoning tithes; and the "new year for the trees," for tree-planting time, still commemorated in Jewish congregations today with the eating of fruit grown in Israel. These were political, economic, or agricultural observances. Rosh Ha-Shanah was set apart as a high holy day, in the fall, to give the year a specifically religious beginning and thus set the spiritual mood for the months ahead.

Creation is the grand, universal motif underlying the colorful rituals and interesting ceremonials that make up the religious celebration of Rosh Ha-Shanah. "Today is the birthday of the world," runs the liturgy, "today, all of the creatures of the world stand in judgment before Thee." So the prayers of Rosh Ha-Shanah are prayers spoken by Jews, not as Jews alone, but as God's creatures, and not for Jews alone, but for all of creation—for all nations and peoples.

The New Year is thus a time of judging, a time for quiet soul-searching and self-examination, to be tremblingly met. This is why one whole month before Rosh Ha-Shanah, at the close of each weekday morning synagogue service, the ram's horn, or shofar, is sounded, a spiritual reveille alerting the community to the New Year at hand and summoning man to put his spiritual affairs in order. For when the awesome day does come, each man must be ready to answer for himself the grave questions posed by the prayer book: "What are we? What is our life? What is our goodness? What is our strength? What is our might? What can we say before Thee, O Lord?"

Then, as the month draws to a close and the new year is about to dawn, a special midnight service of penitence is held on the Saturday preceding Rosh Ha-Shanah. In hushed solemnity the service begins; the voice of the cantor is lifted in supplication pleading for divine forgiveness.

Together, openly and publicly, the entire congregation recites part of the confessional which will be repeated on the Day of Atonement: "We have trespassed . . . we have spoken slander . . . we have scoffed . . ." Always, in Judaism, the confession is made in the form of public prayer, and always the words begin with "we." The individual is answerable for the sins of society.

The theme for the season has already been sounded in the "days of prelude." Now, the day itself arrives. As with all other sacred moments in the Jewish calendar, the home shares with the synagogue responsibility for creating and sustaining the religious mood.

As the sun sets on the last day of the old year, the Jewish mother lights the festival candles symbolically welcoming the new year with the light of faith. Softly, she recites benedictions of gratitude for family blessings and for the gift of life and health in the year just closing.

A step from the ceremonial candelabrum, a proud possession of every Jewish home, stands the "charity box." Whenever the mother lights the tapers on the eve of Sabbaths, festivals, and holy days, she combines the ceremonial with the moral, reverently setting aside something for the less fortunate.

After the candles have been kindled, the father continues the ritual of thanksgiving. Raising a goblet of wine, symbol of life's material bounty, he recites the *Kiddush,* prayer of sanctification, consecrating the family hearth as an altar to the service of God and man. Apples are ceremonially dipped into honey and bitten into, as greetings for a "sweet year" are exchanged.

"May you be inscribed in the Book of Life for a good year!" is a Hebrew phrase literally filling the air in the days between Rosh Ha-Shanah and Yom Kippur wherever Jews meet.

On the New Year, the Book of Life is spread open before the Great Judge. On this day—some understand this literally, others metaphorically—all of the inhabitants of the world pass for judgment before the Creator, as sheep pass for examination before the shepherd. Three books of account are said to be opened on Rosh Ha-Shanah, wherein the fate of the wicked, the righteous, and those in between is recorded. The names of the righteous are immediately inscribed and they are sealed "to live." The wicked are "blotted out of the book of the living." Those in between are given a respite of ten days, from Rosh Ha-Shanah until Yom Kippur—time to repent of their evil ways and to seek the ways of righteousness.

On these days the setting and the spirit is different from the rest of the year. The rabbi and cantor are traditionally robed in white, for white symbolizes the longing for purity of soul and body which is the theme of the season.

The music is penitential in character and the sublime prayers bespeak the significance of the moral life and the beauty of holiness. History seems to hover about the congregation as the worshippers re-enact a ritual which goes back many centuries.

Perhaps it is this spirit of reverence for the ancient tradition which makes the shofar blast so climactic a part of the service. One hundred times the service is punctuated with the sound of the ram's horn, to the accompaniment of Biblical verses which remind the congregation of Israel's covenant with the Lord. Why a ram's horn? The Bible lesson for Rosh Ha-Shanah suggests an answer: Abraham's faith was successfully tested when he showed himself ready at the divine command to sacrifice even Isaac; once the test was passed, a ram was sacrificed in Isaac's stead. The ram is the eternal reminder of the faithfulness of Abraham, and so it is used to recall to his people the faithfulness of the first man to seek the one God. The shrill, quivering notes of the horn are a call to action, reminding the Jew that the Kingdom of God can be realized in one's personal life, even in the midst of the evil of the world in which we live.

The ten-day penitential period moves toward its climax with the coming of the Eve of Atonement.

## Yom Kippur, Day of Atonement

*Yom Kippur,* or the Day of Atonement, comes on the tenth day of Tishri, and it concludes the penitential season. This is the great fast day of the Jewish calendar, and it lasts for twenty-four hours. A public confession of all sins, committed wittingly or unwittingly, is the major theme of the synagogue services. Five separate and complete services, which begin on the evening of the Day of Atonement and end the next nightfall, make up the public observance of this solemn day. The first evening service is said at dusk by a fasting congregation. It is known as *Kol Nidre,* from its first words, which mean "all vows." The "vows" referred to in the *Kol Nidre* are only those which an individual has assumed for himself, voluntarily. Only those oaths of personal conscience, which a man has taken in his aspiration to achieve for himself a moral life, are involved. No promise, oath, or vow which affects the status of another person, a court of law, or a community is implied in this formula of absolution. In many ways, it also operated as a means of self-purgation for Jews, who, living as a persecuted people, were required to swear allegiance to alien gods under penalty of death. Thus, oaths which were extorted from them at the hands of the intolerant, and which reflected their unwilling, but forced adherence to foreign religious beliefs, were annulled in the *Kol Nidre* formula, because they dealt with matters of personal conscience.

Yet, while the *Kol Nidre* serves as an absolution of ceremonial vows, and of oaths relating to religious rituals and customs, this constitutes but a single aspect of its meaning. It was undoubtedly originally introduced into the Atonement liturgy in order to emphasize the way in which a man must prepare for repentance. For, while ritual vows—those made between man and his God—may be annulled, the tradition specifically states that forgiveness for moral trespasses—those actions which encompass man in relationship with his fellow man—can be obtained only when the person who has been aggrieved pardons the offender. The Mishnah states: "For transgressions between man and God, repentance brings atonement. For transgressions between man and man, Yom Kippur brings no atonement, until the injured party is appeased."

A few minutes before sunset, the devotions begin with a solemn declaration pronounced from the rostrum by the rabbi and two learned members of the congregation, each holding a Scroll of the Law in his arms. Then follows the stirring and haunting melody of *Kol Nidre*. The *Kol Nidre* service has been called "the first movement of a devotional symphony which increases in momentum from minute to minute throughout the day."

After the first evening service, the congregation returns home and early the next morning services are resumed. The four services that follow are so arranged that they continue almost without interruption until sunset.

The Great Fast Day comes to a close with the appearance of the first three stars. It has been a long day and there is weariness of body, but the people's spirits have been exalted. Buoyantly and expectantly they come to their feet as a long blast of the shofar marks the end of the fast. "Hear, O Israel, the Lord our God, the Lord is One," they sing out as one, echoing with fervor the monotheistic credo of their father Abraham. And as the shofar is blown, from the lips of every worshipper comes the age-old longing, "May Jerusalem be rebuilt in the year to come!"

### Sukkot, Feast of Tabernacles (Booths)

Five days after Yom Kippur, on the fifteenth of Tishri, the first of the three harvest festivals is celebrated. This is the Feast of Tabernacles (Booths), or *Sukkot,* and it marks the change of moods—from solemnity to joy. In the earliest period of Israel's history, it was known as the Feast of Ingathering, a week-long celebration over the joy of the fall harvest. Indeed, Governor William Bradford of Plymouth Colony patterned the first American Thanksgiving after this old Jewish tradition. But the three harvest festivals were given additional meaning in the course of time, as we have seen. The Feast of Tabernacles was made to signify the gratitude of Israel for God's providence during the forty years of wandering in the wilderness of Sinai. Like Passover and Pentecost, the other two harvest festivals, it came to be related to the major historical event in Israel's life—the redemption from Egypt.

The enriching of the purely agricultural festival of *Sukkot,* by making it into an historical and religious remembrance, was achieved by the rabbis of the Talmud. They interpreted the "booths," the ancient abodes of the Semites, in such a way as to serve as a reminder of the dwelling in which the

Israelites lived when they wandered through the wilderness of Sinai on their journeys from Egypt to the Promised Land.

Thus, the Feast of Tabernacles became a logical sequel to Passover and Pentecost—the first commemorated the release from the bondage of Egypt, the second the receiving of the Law at Sinai.

Outside of Palestine, except among Reform Jews, *Sukkot* is celebrated for eight days. The first and last two days are commemorated by special services in the home and the synagogue. Devout Jews erect a small booth in which they eat their meals throughout the holiday, as a personal reminder of the hardships caused, in part, by the frail huts in which the Israelites dwelled during the years of wandering in the wilderness. The *sukkah,* or booth, has improvised walls and a covering of leafy branches and twigs instead of a roof or ceiling. It must not be lower than five feet, nor higher than thirty, and it must be exposed to a view of the stars. Since it must be re-experienced each year, a permanent sukkah is prohibited.

The harvest side of the holiday is celebrated further by the ceremonial of the *lulav,* a cluster made up of a palm branch, three myrtle twigs, and two willow sprigs. The *lulav* is taken in the right hand, and in the left hand a citron is placed. At certain portions of the service, they are moved to and fro: eastward, southward, westward, northward, upward and downward to symbolize the universal gratitude for the harvest, to the God who is to be found everywhere. As the palm cluster is taken in hand litanies of praise are sung, punctuated by the phrase "Hoshana"—which literally means, in Hebrew, "O save Us!" and which has entered the English language as "hosanna." The use of the palm in the church ritual on "Palm Sunday" has come into Christianity through the doors of Judaism, for palms came to be associated with the theme of "hosanna"—the idea of salvation. When Jesus entered Jerusalem during what has now come to be known as "Holy Week," he was greeted by his followers with palm-branches amidst the shouts of "hoshana"—O save Us! Sometime early in the Middle Ages, the church began to bless and distribute palms on the Sunday before Easter, as a remembrance of the events of Holy Week. As part of the special "Palm Sunday" ritual, the priest of the Roman Catholic Church reads the Old Testament account of the journey of the children of Israel through the wilderness to Mount Sinai where they found twelve springs of water and seventy palm trees.

Thus, the palm branch, used by Jews in the synagogue on *Sukkot* to symbolize their belief in dependence upon God as the God of Nature, has entered into Christianity, and may yet serve Christians as a reminder of their Hebraic past.

On the eighth day, immediately upon the conclusion of *Sukkot,* a one-day festival, known in the Bible as the "Eighth Day of Solemn Assembly," is commemorated. Special prayers for rain mark the services of the day. The long summer season of the Land of Israel is now over, the autumn harvest is in, and now the people and the soil eagerly await the quenching and fructifying rains, which bring comfort and hope to both. Despite the fact that the people of Israel were, until 1948, not masters of their own land, wherever they dwelletl, they retained the ties to their land by means of the special prayers in the synagogue which were established in the earlier days of their history.

### Simhat Torah, Rejoicing in the Law

The very next day there follows a holiday which is not mentioned in the Bible, but which grew up in the Middle Ages. It is the day of "Rejoicing in the Torah," *Simhat Torah.* This is the time when the annual cycle of the public Torah reading is completed, and begun again. Exactly a year before, the weekly reading started with the first chapters of Genesis. Each week, thereafter, consecutive chapters of the Books of Genesis, Exodus, Leviticus, Numbers, and Deuteronomy were ead in the form of a weekly lesson. Now, the time has come o conclude the cycle as the closing verses of Deuteronomy are reached. The services have been made to symbolize the eternal character of the Torah, and so the first chapters of Genesis are read immediately following. Thus, the cycle is never-ending. On this happy occasion, all of the men and children in the synagogue are called up to the reading, singly or in groups, and each one personally rejoices in the Torah. Joy stems from gratitude that God has enabled the congregation to complete and to begin another year of the study of the Torah.

On the eve of *Simhat Torah,* all but one of the Torah Scrolls are removed from the Holy Ark—the Ark must never be left completely empty of Scrolls. These Scrolls are paraded in seven processions around the sanctuary by the male members of the congregation. Heading the "line of march" are usually the children who merrily wave flags inscribed in Hebrew with religious sentiments—various scriptural verses.

On the following morning, the very last and the very first portions of the Pentateuch are read. The reading from Deuteronomy is awarded to a learned member of the congregation who is honorably called the "Bridegroom of the Torah"; the section read from Genesis is similarly awarded, and the man called to the desk for this reading is given the title, "Bridegroom of Genesis."

The Five Books of Moses, or the Pentateuch, are known as a Scroll of the Torah when they are written by hand on parchment and rolled as a scroll. The Scroll, is, of course, written in Hebrew by a pious person known as a scribe. This scribe also writes the parchment strips contained in the *tephillin* and the *mezzuzah.* But his most arduous work, his labor of love, is reserved for the writing of a Scroll of the Torah. This often takes as long as a year, for it must be done according to very careful prescriptions. In the synagogue, the Scroll of the Torah is wrapped in beautiful silk or velvet mantles, and ornamental silver crowns adorn its wooden rollers. When a Torah Scroll is presented to the congregation by a member or a friend, it is an occasion for great rejoicing. Each year, when *Simhat Torah* is celebrated, before the Torah reading all of the Scrolls are removed from the Holy Ark and carried in a happy procession amidst the joyful singing of prayers of thanksgiving. A gay, informal mood envelops the synagogue. For children, particularly, *Simhat Torah* is one of the most beloved of the Jewish festivals. The holiday which celebrates both the completion and commencement of the Reading of the Law is a special day in the lives of Jews, for the Bible is ingrained into the very core of Jewish life.

## Hanukkah, the Feast of Lights

*Hanukkah,* or the Feast of Lights, the last of the autumn holidays in the Jewish calendar, is celebrated for eight days, beginning with the twenty-fifth of Kislev. Until recent years, it was considered to be a minor festival. But in America, perhaps because of its proximity to the holiday of Christmas, Jewish families go to great lengths to make this a joyous time for home celebrations.

The events surrounding the story of *Hanukkah* are related to the victory of the Maccabees over the forces of Antiochus Epiphanes, in 165 B.C.E. This Syrian king had established a pagan altar in the Temple of Jerusalem, and the Jewish way of life was threatened with extinction by his anti-religious decrees. Judas the Maccabee led a small force of devoted followers against outnumbering Syrian armies, and finally succeeded in re-establishing the Temple as a place of Jewish worship. Dedication ceremonies were held, lasting for eight days, following the example of those conducted at the time of the dedication of Solomon's first Temple. From these ceremonies the appropriate symbol of light became associated with the observance of *Hanukkah* as the Feast of Dedication. At home and in the synagogue, a nine-branched candelabra is kindled—different from the one used as a synagogue symbol. With one candle the others are lighted, and each night the lights are increased until on the eighth and last night all nine candles are burning. A home ritual surrounds the lighting of the candelabra, or *menorah,* and every night of the holiday season, parents and children join in the singing of religious hymns and the exchanging of gifts.

It has been suggested that the *Hanukkah* season may have its roots in an ancient pagan institution which commemorated the close of the autumn season and the beginning of winter. Whatever the real origin of the festival, the significance of the holiday for the Jew stems from the heroic story of the Maccabees who fought against mighty odds and succeeded in establishing religious liberty for their people. Perhaps the custom of kindling lights originally arose from a fear-ridden primitive practice performed around the time of the winter solstice, when the days grew short and darkness abounded. But the *Hanukkah* story, in any event, changed this stark meaning into a paean of praise to the God of Israel for the light of faith that is never extinguished.

# XIII The Winter Holidays

## The Fifteenth of Shevat

Jews celebrate the beginning of the religious year in the fall, but they observe still another "New Year" in the winter season. In earlier times, when they still lived principally in Palestine, they set aside the fifteenth day of Shevat as the "New Year for the Trees." Even after they were exiled from their land, they continued to recall this ancient "arbor day," as a bond with their agricultural past. Throughout the lands of their dispersion, in the midst of European winters, when the fifteenth day of Shevat arrived, they recalled that spring was about to come to the land of Israel. It was a day of recollection and of hope. They recalled the land where their fathers once walked, where prophets and sages trod; they hoped that one day this land would again be theirs, even as it had been promised to Abraham. Although they used no rituals on this minor holiday, they symbolized their love for the Holy Land by eating Palestinian fruits and by recalling the agricultural life of the Jews in ancient Palestine.

That a Jew who lived in non-tropical countries should have thought of the coming of spring in a month like February, simply because spring was then about to come to Palestine, helps us to understand the close ties he maintained with the land of his fathers. Nor were these ties political or ecclesiastical. After 70 C.E. there was no Jewish state until the State of Israel came into being in 1948. There was no Temple in Jerusalem either; the synagogue had followed the Jews wherever they went. But throughout the ages, the Jews retained a strong sense of attachment to the land that had cradled their people and which was the scene of the past glories of their heritage. On *Hamishah Asar Bi-Shevat,* the fifteenth day of Shevat, in Jewish homes, this sentiment still comes alive, and with it, the land does, too. Indeed, one cannot fully understand Judaism without taking into account the central religious and cultural role that the Land of Israel plays in Jewish life.

*Purim, the Feast of Lots*

On the fourteenth of Adar (and in leap years, the second Adar), Jews celebrate a jolly holiday which ranks in gaiety with *Simhat Torah*. On *Simhat Torah* Jews are happy because of the Torah. On this holiday of *Purim,* they recall with joy the downfall of Haman, their great oppressor. The story of *Purim* is told in the Book of Esther, found in the third section of Jewish Scripture. Mordecai and Esther are the heroes of the tale, which reads like a modern-day suspense story. Haman, vizier of King Ahasuerus, had plotted to kill all the Jews of the Persian empire. But the heroes saved the day. Haman was foiled and was hung from the very gallows he had prepared for Mordecai. He had chosen the fourteenth day of Adar as the day when he would annihilate all of the Jews of the empire. Instead of becoming a day of mourning it became a day of joy. *Purim* is also known as the Feast of Lots, because Haman had selected the extermination date by casting lots.

This happy holiday is commemorated in the synagogue by the public reading of the Book of Esther both at the evening and morning service. The reading is customarily accompanied by the excited stamping of feet and the happy sounding of noisemakers at every mention of Haman's name. In many Jewish homes the day is also celebrated by a festive meal, highlighted by a masquerade consisting of the characters of the *Purim* story. *Purim* is thus a folk festival, sounding a note of light relief, and leavening the religious year with the elements of fun and merriment. It marks the close of the winter holidays for the Jew. Four weeks later spring will begin, when the dramatic holiday season of Passover arrives.

# XIV The Spring Holidays

## Passover

The theme of Passover runs through all of Jewish religious life like a silver cord. Every Sabbath eve, during the prayers that accompany the festive meal, the Exodus from Egypt is recalled. And, again, on every major festival of the year, there is a remembrance of the wonderful deliverance which God wrought for the Israelites when He redeemed them from Egypt. The Jewish prayer-book refers to this divine liberation from bondage many more times than it does to any other single event in Jewish history. For Judaism is a God-centered civilization and Passover celebrates God the redeemer. The redeeming God, for the Jew, is pure spirit, and His works are known through the events of history. When the grip of winter is broken and nature is being resurrected, Passover comes. It is the first of the spring festivals, and on the night of spring's first full moon its celebration begins. Nature, too, is being released from its thralldom, even as the Israelites had gained their freedom from servitude. The new young grain sticking its head through the fertile earth is a reminder of life's rebirth.

With the two other harvest festivals, Tabernacles and Pentecost, Passover celebrates God in nature as well as history. In the twelfth chapter of the Book of Exodus there is a detailed description of the manner in which the Passover was first celebrated. At the full moon of the first month of spring, every family slaughtered a lamb or a goat at twilight. In the middle of the night they ate it in common, together with unleavened bread and bitter herbs. The meal had to be eaten in haste, and whatever was not consumed had to be burned before the break of dawn. After the slaughtering, hyssop was dipped into the animal's blood, and a few drops were sprinkled with it on the doorposts of each house. This was known as the ceremony of *Pesach,* the paschal lamb. For a full week thereafter, a Festival of Unleavened Bread was celebrated and no fermented food (*hametz*) was permitted to be eaten In this way the early Israelites celebrated the first rites of spring.

But when they were liberated from Egypt, that great experience left an indelible mark upon their spirit. The older ritual of *Pesach* was taken over and given a new significance. All of the elements of these ceremonies were now invested with the new meanings associated with liberation from Egyptian bondage. Passover now referred to the time that God "passed over" the houses of the Israelites when he came to destroy the Egyptian first-born. The unleavened bread became a memorial of the hurried departure from Egypt—there had been no time to wait for the dough to rise, and so the bread was baked without leavening. In short order, the historical significance of Passover as commemorating the Exodus, and its meaning as a festival of freedom, completely overshadowed the earlier agricultural phase of the holiday.

The rabbis of the Talmud prescribed a number of regulations, based upon their interpretation of Scripture, which were designed to emphasize these new meanings. Jews were required to eat *matzah,* or unleavened bread, throughout the festival period, as a reminder of the bread of poverty which their ancestors had eaten when they were slaves in the land of Egypt. The scrupulous avoidance of eating any food on this holiday that has come in contact with leavening or certain kinds of grain is also intended as a reminder of the food the Israelites ate when they were liberated. The motive behind these ritual precautions is principally educational: each Jewish home must relive the Exodus, so that it may come to know the greatness of God's redeeming powers. "For God did not redeem our ancestors alone, but us, as well," runs a prayer of the Passover home ritual. In this way, the Exodus becomes an ongoing process, for God's liberating power is unending.

This Jewish Feast of Unleavened Bread—*matzot*—has left its mark on Christianity, as well. Easter was originally (and in some sections of Christendom still is) called "the pascha," thus associating it with the paschal lamb which the ancient Israelites slaughtered on the eve of Passover. Additionally, the bread used as the Host in the Roman Catholic Mass—a thin, circular wafer—must be unleavened, for the assumption is that the bread to which Jesus referred at his Last Supper was actually *matzah,* since it was presumed to be a Passover meal. Protestants, however, at their Holy Communion services use leavened bread because they follow a tradition established by the Greek Orthodox Church in 1043, when it overthrew a number of the older traditions of the church.

Orthodox and Conservative Jews in America celebrate Passover for eight days, and the Reform group observes it for one week. But while major public services are conducted on the first and last two days of the festival, the Jewish home is the real center of Passover observance. On the first two evenings of the holiday, a special ritual meal known as a *seder* (meaning "order of service"), is conducted at the family table. Every member of the family participates in the ritual and is supplied with a copy of the Passover *haggadah,* a special prayer book containing the various ceremonies and readings connected with the celebration of the *seder.* In the center of the table are placed the cakes of *matzah;* the bitter herbs; a roasted egg, to symbolize the ancient sacrifice; parsley, as a green sign of spring's coming; and a mixture of apples, nuts and wine called *haroset,* made to look like the mortar used by the Israelites as slave-builders of the store-cities of the Egyptian Pharaohs. At various points in the ritual meal, these foods are consumed and their symbolical meanings are explained. Many of these explanations are given with the children in mind, for they are very much a part of this family service. In response to the youngest child's "Four Questions," an old ritual formula having a pedagogical motivation, the father recounts the narrative story of the Exodus. The *seder* concludes as all join in singing many joyous hymns. Passover helps to make the family, through its shared table ritual, into a warm and glowing community.

## Shavuot, or Pentecost

The closing spring festival of the Jewish calendar falls seven weeks after the beginning of Passover. In Hebrew, therefore, it is known as *Shavuot,* or the Feast of Weeks. Because it falls on the fiftieth day, following Passover, it has also come to be known as Pentecost, which in Greek means "fifty." The weeks which separate these two harvest festivals are called the Days of the Omer, named after the Hebrew word meaning "sheaf." Sheaves of barley, the first crop to ripen, were offered as a Temple sacrifice on the second night of Passover. Thereafter, the farmers counted each day, expectantly waiting for the fiftieth day, at which time the major crops would be ready for harvesting. Then, on the fiftieth day, amidst great rejoicing, they brought the first pickings of their fruits and grains to the Temple, as another offering to God in gratitude for the bounty of their harvest.

During the time of the rabbis, both the Days of the Omer and Pentecost underwent changes in meaning. The Omer days became a time of partial mourning, a kind of lenten period. Marriages were not solemnized, new clothes could not be worn, hair could not be cut, nor was public entertainment permitted. Except for Sabbaths and new moons, some of these restrictions were lifted on only one day—the thirty-third day. The precise reasons for all of this are difficult to determine. Jewish tradition explains that the Omer days became days of partial mourning because of the plague which killed the disciples of Rabbi Akiba, a foremost scholar and teacher, and which abated only for one day—the thirty-third day. Orthodox Jews still observe this period in the traditional fashion, although most Conservative and Reform Jews do not.

The rabbis reinterpreted the significance of Pentecost in a way that has been most important for Jewish religious life. Again we see how they understood the work of God in history. Their interpretation of the meaning of Pentecost hinges upon their understanding of the purposes of the Exodus. God did not deliver the Israelites from Egypt just to rescue them from bondage, important as that may have been. Liberation from Egypt was linked to a spiritual purpose. God freed Israel, so that as free men they could serve Him. But how should Israel serve God, asked the rabbis? The answer they gave is implied in the way they reinterpreted Pentecost. By revealing His Law to them, God would teach Israel how to do His will. Thus, Pentecost became the great festival of Revelation, commemorating the giving of the Law on Sinai. In the synagogue, this idea is highlighted in the Scriptural lesson chosen for the holiday. From the Book of Exodus, chapters are read which describe the dramatic story of Mount Sinai and the promulgation of the Ten Commandments. In many congregations in America, as a link to the Torah, Pentecost has been fittingly selected as the day when Confirmation services are held for the graduates of the synagogue religious school.

As the spring cycle comes to a close, the Torah again becomes the center of Jewish life. Without the Torah even the Exodus would be meaningless.

Ever since Paul replaced the Jewish idea of Torah with the Christian concept of the Messiah-Savior, at best, the Torah could be viewed as only a "schoolmaster to bring us to Christ." As a result, the Christian church could not take over those earlier Jewish practices which gave special and central significance to the place of the Law in the life of the spirit. The Jewish Festival of Pentecost, *Shavuot,* is an obvious case in point, for it was made to commemorate the giving of the Law at Sinai. And yet, old Jewish habits died hard in the nascent Christian Church. The early Christians still wanted to celebrate this festival—but to do so and still follow the Pauline teachings, they had to give it new and different content. This they did by linking the festival of Pentecost to the death of Jesus (as they had, in a way, done with the Jewish Passover) rather than continuing its original Jewish associations with the Torah. As the Feast of Weeks fell on the fiftieth day after Passover, so the Christian festival of Pentecost was made to fall on the fiftieth day following Easter Sunday. This was arrived at by means of the following chronology: Following the Resurrection of Jesus on Easter Sunday, forty days ensued until his Ascension heavenward. In the remaining ten days the Apostles waited until Jesus, from Heaven, sent them the Holy Ghost. On the fiftieth day, or what now became the Christian Feast of Pentecost, the Holy Ghost descended. While the Christian Pentecost now was observed at the same time as the Jewish Pentecost, it no longer had the earlier significance; now, as the day when the Holy Ghost descended from Heaven, it marked the birthday of the church on earth.

Thus, the Jewish holiday, *Shavuot,* which celebrates the pre-eminent place of the Law in Jewish religious life, has, for Christians, become the very day which saw the establishment of the Church as a divine institution. Just as the Law of the Torah—for Jews—is divine, and therefore above all else the essence of Judaism, so, for Christians, the Church is the divine instrument for the realization of religious fulfillment.

Paraphrasing Paul, we note again: The synagogue in itself is not divine; it is but a schoolhouse to bring the Jew, and the world, closer to an understanding of the teachings of the Moral Law and the commandments.

## xv The Summer Holidays

### The Ninth Day of Av

The summer months of the Jewish calendar have relatively few days of ritual significance. The principal commemoration turns on the mournful remembrance of Jerusalem's destruction, and the loss of the Temple. Tradition records that the First Temple was destroyed in the sixth century B.C.E., on the ninth day of the month of Av. Some six hundred and fifty-five years later, the Romans destroyed the Second Temple on the very same date. Small wonder, then, that this date is observed in a spirit of mourning.

The observance of the Ninth of Av has been transformed from a single day into a season. Three weeks before it is reached, on the seventeenth of Tammuz, the mood is established. It was on the seventeenth day of Tammuz, in 70 C.E., that the Romans made the first breach in the Temple walls, and this led to the final destruction three weeks later. During this three-week period, no marriages are solemnized by Orthodox or Conservative rabbis, and public entertainment is avoided by traditional Jews. In the synagogue, on the three Sabbaths preceding the Ninth of Av, selections which describe the impending doom of Jerusalem, are read from the Prophets. When the eve of the fateful day finally comes, the synagogue is plunged into mourning. The veil before the Holy Ark is removed, and seated on a low stool, as a mourner, the synagogue reader chants the five chapters of the Book of Lamentations in dirge-like style. Traditional Jews fast for twenty-four hours from sunset to sunset, as a sign of their personal participation in the sorrows of Jewish history.

But soon consolation is offered. The seven Sabbaths preceding the Jewish New Year are known as the Sabbaths of Consolation, and on those days special consolatory sections are read from the Prophets. Thus, the season that follows the fast of the Ninth of Av is a kind of preface to the New Year, offering hope and comfort.

When the New Year comes, the summer period has ended,

and the fall cycle begins once again. In the fall of 1984, for example, Jews celebrated the year 5745. According to Jewish tradition, creation took place in September or October of 3761 B.C.E. To be sure, this calculation is not based upon scientific fact, nor for that matter, does it have any dogmatic sanction in Judaism. Rabbi Jose ben Halafta, a Palestinian rabbi of the second century C.E., had arrived at this calculation on the basis of knowledge then available to him. Since his time, Jews have followed his rather arbitrary figure as the basis for numbering their years. It is interesting to note, however, that Jews use the creation of the world as the starting point in the calendar, while Christians and Moslems reckon the years from the lifetime of the founders of their religion.

*PART IV* SACRED IDEAS

# XVI Of God and Man

Martin Buber, eminent Jewish philosopher, asks the Christian the fundamental question: "What have you and we in common?"

His question, however, is not motivated by the vulgar or pseudo-liberal expectation of answers which suggest that all differences are superficial. If so, the question is really unworthy, for it produces an intellectual evasion. If, when we ask, we really do not care to know, neither analysis nor insight is possible. To arrive at a synthesis of understanding, we must seek to plumb the meanings of antithesis.

Thus, Buber answers by suggesting that what is ultimately common is the result of that which is fundamentally different. In common, he says, we have a book and an expectation. "To you, the book is a forecourt; to us, it is the sanctuary . . . Your expectation is directed toward a second coming, ours to a coming which has not been anticipated by a first. It behooves both you and us to hold inviolably fast to our own true faith, that is, to our own deepest relationships to truth. . . . Our task is not to tolerate each other's waywardness, but to acknowledge the real relationship in which both stand to the truth."

Buber's point is well made: Judaism and Christianity are uniquely paired; they are posed in a fundamental relationship to each other despite their separate interpretations of religious truth. As far as Christianity is concerned Judaism can never be looked upon as being *just* another minority religion. For these two religions confront each other in continuing dialogue: the face of one is constantly set against the other in historic encounter.

Hellenism and Hebraism were the essential traditions which molded Christian thought of God and man. But, if Christians choose now to dismiss Judaism and its monotheism, they do so at the peril of falling back into the pre-Christian pagan Greek-mysteries in whose spiritual soil so much of early Christian theology was also imbedded. Hellenism no longer possesses a living, vital center out of which to challenge, criticize, or refine Christian teaching. But Judaism still survives as a dynamic religion. Thus, Christians cannot avoid the dialogue with Judaism. Even if Christianity closes its eyes to this, the dialogue continues; the encounter cannot be waved off because Judaism continues to thrive. Ultimately, we should not merely "tolerate each other's waywardness," but rather learn to acknowledge the meaning of our differences. Only then is there validity to the many things we do share in common.

As part of the public worship of most Christian churches, the Creeds which form the basis of their theological platforms are regularly recited. While all Christians share the Apostles' Creed, many of the denominations have added their own confessions—as, for example, the Lutherans have the Augsburg Confession and the Presbyterians, the Westminster Confession. The liturgy of the churches is shaped and molded by their adherence to these special theological formulations. The Creeds of the various churches have become the foundation of the whole super-structure of their belief, because most Christian churches and denominations originated as doctrinal associations of like-minded believers. Some declaration of faith, some official credo, some specific articulation of belief marked these groups off, at the very outset of their historic careers, as uniquely differentiated from their neighbors. This explains why many of these movements, like Christianity itself, are named for their founders, who formulated a guiding set of theological principles in order to establish these groups as distinct from any others. Christianity is named for Christ; and so with Lutheranism, Calvinism, Zwinglianism, Wesleyanism, and many others.

At a synagogue service, however, one does not hear a recitation or public proclamation of *the Jewish creed*. The reason for this is simple: A single, official synagogue creed does not exist. Judaism, as its name suggests, is the religious civilization of *the Jewish people*—and congregants of a synagogue are more than members of a church organized by a founder in order to propagate a particular theological formulation. For Jews did not adopt Judaism in the way in which Romans and others once converted to Christianity or, as one may today, adopt the religion of the Baptist Church after leaving another. Jews created Judaism—they were not converted to it. They molded and shaped a way of life, belief, and practice which grew organically out of their group life—and this has come to be known as Judaism. And so, while Judaism has its own unique attitudes about God, its theological systems have never been compactly or officially ordered, arranged, or defined. Judaism has been relatively free from the authoritative or dogmatic theological coercions of a central religious body, and Jews have been privileged to enjoy wide latitude in defining and crystallizing their concepts of God.

Earlier, we indicated that while Judaism has been called a religion of ethical monotheism, it is more properly understood as a way of life based upon a Jewish system of *monotheistic ethics*. The Law, or Torah, contains the essential precepts whereby the Jew is helped to know God—not by abstract or mystical faith alone, but rather through a serious attempt to conform to the Divine plan for human behavior. These commandments are 613 in number and they run the gamut of personal, interpersonal, and social relations. While logically a belief in a God who reveals His will to man is at the core of this system, the rabbinic compilers of the 613 Biblical precepts nowhere listed "belief in God" as one of these commandments. They understood "belief" in the peculiarly Jewish meaning of the word; no man could be commanded to believe abstractly and no human tribunal could punish him for not believing. The Jew accepts "God's Kingdom" by building it on earth. In a fairly remarkable piece of Biblical exegesis, a Talmudic rabbi resoundingly summed up the Jewish position: "In the book of Jeremiah it is written: For thus saith the Lord of Hosts, the God of Israel: 'Me have they forsaken and they have not kept My law.' This is what

[135]

God is really saying: 'Would that men forsook Me, if only they kept My law!' "

From this insight into the Jewish understanding of God's purposes, we recognize that Judaism conceived of the "Kingdom of God" quite differently from the way in which Christians later conceived of it. In Judaism's view, the Kingdom of God (*malchut shamayim*) is definitely of *this* world, and man's tasks and responsibilities are centered *here*. The Hebrew word for "kingdom" (*malchut*) does not imply spatial, or political territory; it is neither a place, nor a world. Indeed, we truly absorb its original significance if, instead of using the word "kingdom," we substitute "kingship," or "sovereignty." Judaism never saw the establishment of the Kingdom of God as a supernatural event which will come to pass when this world withers away and the Future World, the Hereafter, is divinely ushered in. Christianity with its emphasis upon the second coming of Jesus, took over this Jewish doctrine with its *this-worldly, ethical* emphasis, and gave it an *other-worldly, mystical* significance. In Judaism, the Kingdom, or Sovereignty of God is realized with the establishment of the Good Society; thus, the rabbis saw God as more concerned that men should follow His Law, than that they should mystically long to commune with Him. And for quite the opposite reason Christianity, pinning its hopes upon a Future World "with the coming of the Kingdom," urges men to seek life eternal through *the only* way to God—through Jesus, the son.

But the indivisible unity of God is the cornerstone of Jewish faith. If Judaism may be said to have a dogmatic theological position, it would certainly rest upon this principle religious conviction. While every generation in Jewish history was free to embellish this basic "dogma" in ways which reflected current concerns, the fundamental principle remained unchanged and uncompromised. Maimonides, twelfth century Jewish physician and rabbi, clearly delineated the classical Jewish view when he said: "I believe with perfect faith that the Creator, blessed be His name, has no bodily form, and that no form can represent Him."

The complete spirituality of God, the utter impossibility of imagining Him in corporeal form, has resulted in a number of specifically Jewish patterns of worship, of important "do's" and "don'ts," which find their way into synagogue life. The so-called "pictureless barrenness" of Jewish congregations, in which the human form may not be graphically portrayed, is a reflection of the disinclination of Judaism to suggest, even remotely, that God has become man, or that man has become God. No men, therefore, have been elevated to the rank of saints in Judaism, for fear that they may be venerated in a way which should be reserved only for God. Even Moses, Law-giver and leader of the Exodus, is accorded no supra-human status by Jews. Indeed, his name has been significantly omitted from the Passover *haggadah,* and the redemption of the Israelites from Egypt is commemorated each year without so much as a pause to give special mention to the man who led the line of march toward freedom. Again, emphasis is placed upon God as the redeemer, who does not become incarnate in any man—not even in Moses. In like fashion, none of the festivals in the Hebrew calendar glorifies the persons of any of the heroes of Jewish history. Always attention is turned away from the human and transient characters who filled the stage of past events, and who were, in effect, only playing a temporary role in the divine drama.

In this connection, it may be well to remember the succinct remark that the "religion *of* Jesus was Judaism, whilst the religion *about* Jesus is Christianity." Jesus lived and died a Jew, and as such, he, like other Jews before and after, participated in religious worship which devoutly followed the Judaic patterns of piety. After the death of Jesus, when Christianity developed as an offshoot from Judaism, the followers of this new religion, in recognition of the life led by Jesus, adopted most of the Jewish festivals he had celebrated—but now gave each of them new meanings which were associated with his death. In this way, the Christian calendar came to be divided into two parts—half of the year is spent in commemorating events which surround the divine birth of Jesus, while the other six months are devoted to festivals and sacred celebrations related to his death and resurrection.

## Resurrection and Immortality

The belief in the resurrection of the dead is one of the chief doctrines of the Christian faith. Without it, much of the structure of Christian belief would collapse. Paul, himself, stated this idea quite unmistakably: "But if there is no resurrection of the dead, then Christ has not been raised; if Christ has not been raised, then our preaching is in vain and your faith is in vain" (I Cor. 15:13). But if one were to seek a report in the Hebrew Bible of the after-life of the great ones—like Abraham, Isaac, Jacob, Moses, Aaron, David, and Solomon—his search would be in vain. In the words of one scholar, "death is a matter of comparative indifference in the Old Testament. Life goes on, and death can not seriously retard its progress through the centuries of history." It is clear that in the Judaism of the Bible serious efforts must have been made to move the attention of man away from preoccupations with death and the dead, from necromancy and spirit divinations, and from the rites of ancestor-worship.

Sometime around the beginning of the Christian Era, concepts of resurrection and immortality, popular among the peoples of the Near East, entered into rabbinic Judaism. Theretofore, longings for immortal life among the Jews had been satisfied by the belief that the individual would find his fulfillment by merging his personal destiny with the immortal life of his people. Now, as a result of the influence of certain Persian and Greek teachings, the rabbis adopted a message: a promise of a happy ending following man's earthly existence—in time and in eternity. But they never rejected this world in their acceptance of another world—they embraced both!

Yet, it was not easy to find clear Biblical warrant for other-worldly concepts. On the contrary—scattered throughout the Scriptures are thoughts which seem to deny these: "The heavens are the Lord's heavens, but the earth He has given to the sons of men. The dead do not praise the Lord, nor do any that go down into silence. But we will bless the Lord from this time forth and evermore" (Ps. 115:16–18). The strong emphasis upon the Torah as the *living* Torah—a way of *life*—and not as a preamble or key to life-after-death, remained predominant, even when the doctrines of resurrection and immortality were given sanction by the rabbis. Thus, the details and forms of the hereafter—of Heaven and Hell—were never officially spelled out, and individual Jews were given free reign to interpret these broadly or narrowly, as their private judgment saw fit. Over-speculation upon the life hereafter, it was feared by the rabbis, might lead to an obsession with the mysteries of other-worldliness; therefore they continued to teach that "better is one hour of repentance and good works in this world than the whole life of the world to come." While recognizing a belief in doctrines of resurrection and immortality, the rabbis, nevertheless, continued to place religious emphasis upon this world—to make this earth and this society a good and congenial abode for both body and the spirit of man. Literal conceptions of Heaven or Hell were discouraged, and as a result, most Jews came to think of them in allegorical rather than concrete terms.

What is generally agreed upon is the belief that death is not the end of life—man's soul is immortal and in the spiritual realms of the Infinite, men live on. Jewish theology, however, is relatively agnostic as to the actual nature of the world to come, and generally is willing to leave the question to God for final resolution. Since Judaism does not rise or fall as it vindicates or fails to justify this belief, its leading thinkers have never been preoccupied with problems connected with after-life. They have a basic faith that in God's universe nothing precious is ever lost—beyond this fundamental conviction they have never officially elaborated a final and complete system of other-worldly salvation.

## Sin

We have already pointed out that Judaism does not possess sacraments, and that its rituals are embodied in symbols which are essentially *educational*, rather than *mystical*. While discussing Jewish ideas of God and man, it becomes necessary to explain in greater detail the crucial reasons for this situation. The ceremonials and rituals which take place in the synagogue or the Jewish home are the visible symbols which are reminiscent of the covenant God made with Israel; they are visible memorials of a history in which God chose them to be the Messiah-people, the moral and religious teachers of mankind. But they are not sacraments. And why not? A sacrament is not a symbol, memorial, or historic reminder; it is the physical incarnation of a belief which saves men. Judaism does not believe in "beliefs" which save men. For the Jew, there are no ceremonial acts whose performance bestows supernatural grace and endows man with the saving power of the divine.

But why does Judaism insist that there are no beliefs which in themselves can save men, and why has Christianity been so adamant in its espousal of the central theme of its faith: Believe in Jesus, and be saved? This question hinges on the problem of Original Sin, and the manner in which Judaism and Christianity view the essential structure of human nature. Judaism centers its message upon the need to fulfill the Law and the Commandments because it applies itself to the challenge of helping men to face up to and over-come their *specific* errors and their *individual* misdeeds. The Confessional of the Day of Atonement, therefore, summons the Jew to a specific awareness of these errors, by enumerating them, *one by one*. In Judaism, there is no adherence to a doctrine which claims man's *general* depravity as the child of Adam; men may err but mankind is not eternally doomed through inheritance of Original Sin. Hebrew Scripture sums up the attitude: "And now, Israel, what does the Lord require of you, but to revere the Lord your God, to walk in His ways, to love Him, to serve the Lord your God with all your heart and with all your soul, and to keep the commandments and statutes of the Lord which I command you this day for your good" (Deut. 10:12–13).

To be sure, Judaism is no Pollyanna looking at the world through rose-colored glasses. It recognizes that man does sin, being aware of his *evil inclination* (*yetzer ha-ra*), even from the time of his youth (Gen. 8:21). But it is equally mindful of man's *good inclination* (*yetzer ha-tov*), and always the emphasis is upon repentance—which it understands as a "return" to the Law of God. And God is seen as patiently awaiting man's return, even until the last moment of his life. Thus atonement cannot be achieved through the vicarious works, faith, or suffering of another. Because it cannot accept the idea of Original Sin, and because repentance is something which each man must seek on his own by returning to God's Law, Judaism has found no need to believe in a mediating redeemer other than God, or a Savior who suffers vicariously in order to bring salvation to otherwise doomed sinners. Nowhere in Hebrew Scriptures were the Jews required to atone for an inherited burden of guilt. In the ancient Temple, no sacrifices were required of them to expiate Original Sin. Again and again, stress is placed on the belief that "*whosoever* hath sinned" shall suffer the consequences of *his own wrongdoing*. To make this point abundantly clear, the rabbis selected the Book of Jonah as the special Scriptural reading for the afternoon service of the Day of Atonement. In that classical gem of universalistic thought, Jews were reminded that God awaits the return of all people—even the people of Nineveh, who had oppressed Israel—and offers them forgiveness if only they leave their unjust ways and accept the moral law of God. And thus of Nineveh, ancient symbol of urban wickedness, the Book of Jonah can say: "And God saw their *works,* that they turned from their *evil way;* and God repented of the evil, which He said He would do unto them; and He did it not" (Jonah 3:10). This is in keeping with other Scriptural teachings. Says Isaiah: "Let the wicked man forsake his way and the bad man his plans, and let him return to the Lord, and He will have mercy upon him" (55:7). And Ezekiel agrees: "As I live saith the Lord, I do not desire the death of the wicked man, but that the wicked man turn from his evil way and live" (33:11).

Repentance, in Judaism, is based essentially upon a moral decision—to return to the Law of God, and the abandonment of evil deeds and intentions. It is linked to a radical change of personal conduct and motivation. Thus, the rabbis of the Talmud set up nine norms of repentance—corresponding to the nine days which intervene between Rosh Ha-Shanah and Yom Kippur—which they took from the nine exhortations God utters in the first chapter of Isaiah: "Wash you, make you pure, remove the evil of your misdeeds from before My eyes, cease doing evil, learn to do well, seek after justice, relieve the oppressed, do justice to the orphan, take up the cause of the widow." What is written after this, the rabbis queried? And, quoting further, they replied: "Come now, let us argue the matter, saith the Lord: if your sins be like scarlet, they shall become white as snow." In the view of the rabbis, then, the *moral* reformation which the prophet Isaiah demanded of the whole people was made into the very means whereby each individual who had sinned, could achieve religious regeneration, by a combination of his own will and God's mercy.

In a profound sense, then, in Judaism, faith is centered not only in God, but also in man. From the very opening chapter of the Book of Genesis, the outlook is one of moral and cosmic optimism: "God saw all that He had made, and behold, it was very good" (Gen. 1:31). This basic affirmation is pronounced over and again throughout the annals of Jewish thought over the years. Sin and evil are dealt with realistically, but without morbidity. They exist and partake of the work of the Creator, but they, too, are capable of serving a moral purpose in life. Essentially, Judaism does not deal with the mysterious meaning of evil by suggesting a theological retreat from life's problems in an escape to a perfect world to come. It may not always satisfy the impatient, for it does not offer glib solutions to what are, in fact, inscrutable problems. The easy way out is not to be found, for Judaism is more concerned with the way in which we approach problems and the manner in which we live *with* them, than with final, neat, and all-embracing solutions. Characteristically, in Hebrew—*mussar*—the word for "suffering," is synonymous with "moral instruction." What we do with the evils which beset us—the moral lessons we learn from them—spell out, perhaps, the very purpose of sin and suffering in the world.

Christianity, on the other hand, sees all sin as related to Original Sin, and not necessarily the result of immoral action on the part of the individual. "In Adam's fall, we sinned all," it maintains. Thus, the need for grace through mediation by a divine person who has not sinned. Therefore, in all of its denominational forms, Christianity has emerged as a sacramental religion—because only a faith in the perfect, mediating Savior can redeem man from the eternal inheritance as well as the ultimate damnation of sin. Then, only, may forgiveness and justification come. In Judaism, however, belief in God is demonstrated by living in accordance with His

[143]

moral law; a man's spiritual life is not completely comprehended by his faith, it only begins with faith. From faith, he must go on to the fulfillment of faith—to a life of ethical conduct based upon the Law. This explains why rituals in Judaism are essentially educational or moral in character, and why sacraments were never introduced into the Jewish religion. Instead, the love of God has been translated from mystical belief into a method of living and into specific modes of behavior. Because of this, "the love of God" can be experienced, not merely by means of theological creed, but through moral instruction and application.

## Justice and Love—God's Dual Attributes

Very often, however, the Jewish concept of Law has been misunderstood to include only the justice and not the mercy and love of God. This is not merely the result of a faulty translation of the Hebrew word *Torah* as "Law," when it really means "teaching," "moral guidance," "ethical instruction." In the first Christian centuries, when Judaism and Christianity were strongly competitive rivals, it became popular and accepted in Church circles to describe the God of the Old Testament as a vengeful Lord of justice, in contrast to the "God of Love" of the New Testament. Objective scholars of both the Jewish and the Christian traditions now realize, however, that no such neat and facile categorization can stand the test of historical truth. If purely statistical evidence were to be made the canon of judgment, a list of divine attributes in the Hebrew Bible which describe God's love and mercy would far outbalance any which speak of unyielding justice. Closer to the truth is the fact that in Judaism God is both just and merciful; He is a righteous God, and a loving God, at one and the same time. This is the "Law"—the Torah—and the equating of this "Law" or "teaching" of Judaism with a stern, wrathful, immutable, and untempered justice, is neither correct nor objective.

At every daily synagogue service, passages from the Bible are read which speak of God as a God of love and mercy: "Thou, O Lord, art a God full of compassion and gracious; low to anger and plenteous in mercy and truth" (Ps. 86: 15). "O give thanks unto the Lord, for He is good; for His mercy endureth forever" (Ps. 136). "The Lord is good to all; and His tender love is over all His works . . . The Lord upholdeth all that fall; and raiseth up all those that are bowed down . . . The Lord is nigh unto all them that call upon Him; to all who call upon Him in truth . . ." (Ps. 145). Indeed, scarcely a page of the *siddur,* the Hebrew prayer book, does not include some reference to the dual attributes—justice and love—by which the God of Israel is known and worshipped in the synagogue.

In dealing with this question, reference should be made to the manner in which the ancient Hebrew law of "an eye for an eye" has been both misunderstood and misappropriated. Long before Shakespeare's "Merchant of Venice" characterized Shylock as exacting his "pound of flesh"—fixing upon justice of this sort as an anti-Semitic stereotype—other would-be detractors of Judaism referred to this Hebrew law of retaliation (*lex talionis*) as an example of the cruelty and barbarism of the Jewish concept of justice.

Three basic pieces of data are necessary, however, in order to view history with proper perspective: First, the Hebrew law of "an eye for an eye" was, in fact, a great social and legal advance in its time. Other ancient peoples viewed such offenses as capital crimes. They did not requite "an eye for an eye," an "arm for an arm," or "a tooth for a tooth." In their "legal systems," they demanded a life for an eye, an arm, or a tooth.

Second, there is literary evidence to indicate that the Biblical law was interpreted—surely by the Pharisees, but even long before their time—to imply a legal principle of damages, rather than an act of physical retaliation. In other words, in actuality, the law was used as a guide for practical application: the *value* of an eye, for the *value* of an eye; the guilty one had to pay the injured man a fair indemnity for the loss of one of his limbs or bodily organs.

Finally, it is highly questionable whether, throughout the history of organized rabbinical religious courts in Palestine, any capital crimes which came before them for judgment were indeed punished by the death sentence—although, the Biblical warrant of a "life for a life" made this permissive. The Pharisees put down legal conditions in cases dealing with capital crimes, with which it was virtually impossible to comply. To cite but one example: If the twenty-three rabbi-judges who made up the tribunal voted unanimously to apply the death sentence, it was ruled that the defendant must be *acquitted!* How so? It was felt that if no extenuating circumstances could be found by just *one* of the twenty-three judges, the trial must have been carried out with a willful prejudice against the defendant! Perhaps this is why the rabbis of the Talmud were quoted as saying that a tribunal dealing in capital crimes which meted out the death sentence *once in seven years,* is called a "court of violence and destruction."

Now, perhaps, it will be better understood why the Pharisees interpreted the two Hebrew names by which God is known in the Bible in the special way in which they did. The two primary names for God, in Scripture, are *YHVH* (*Yahweh*) and *Elohim.* Interpreting the verse in Genesis (2:4), "In the day that the Lord God (*YHVH Elohim*) made heaven and earth," the Talmud said: "To what may this be compared? It may be compared to a king who had empty glasses. He said: 'If I pour hot water into them they will crack; if I pour cold water into them they will also crack!' What did the king do? He mixed the hot and the cold water together and poured it into them and they did not crack. Even so did the Holy One blessed be He, say: 'If I create the world on the basis of the attribute of mercy alone, the world's sins will multiply greatly. If I create it on the basis of the attribute of justice alone, how could the world endure? Therefore, I will create it with both the attributes of mercy and justice, and may it endure!' " Thus did the Pharisees understand God to possess both the attributes of justice (*middat ha-din*) *and* mercy (*middat ha-rahamim*) as *YHVH* and as *Elohim*.

And yet, while the rabbis of the Talmud spoke of these two attributes of God, the tendency in Judaism from the time of Maimonides on has been to desist from speculating too much on what God *is*. Maimonides and his fellow medieval Jewish philosophers were most reluctant to describe God in terms of human attributes at all. They felt that a pure monotheism could not support a definition of God which tended to humanize or personify Him. All that man can really know about God, they taught, is what He *is not*. Any ascription to God of positive attributes would result, they believed, in a dilution of Judaism's highly spiritualized theology; it would lead to a materialization of the Infinite. God, in relation to man, is so transcendent, so totally other, that for man to know Him completely, man would have to possess divine qualities. More important, they taught, is it for man to try to understand what *God does, not what God is*. In this sense, they were not speculative philosophers, as much as religious existentialists, who were concerned with the human and humane effects which an exalted monotheism might produce in the life of the active believer.

But if God is transcendent and totally other, if He cannot be completely known or visualized, how can man even begin to approach Him, to know Him as a loving Father? In much the same way in which Judaism resolves a seeming paradox by combining the justice of God with His mercy, so it melds the idea of an Omnipotent King of the Universe, with a belief in a God Who can be intimately addressed by His worshippers as "Thou." Every time a Jew pronounces a benediction—at home, in the synagogue, or anywhere he may find himself—the very formula of the blessing seeks to resolve the paradox. He can intimately praise the God of Creation as his very own, personal God. When, for example, he partakes of food, he recites: "Praised be *Thou,* O Lord *our* God, King of the *Universe,* Who bringest forth bread from the earth." Three ideas of God are incorporated in this, as in every other Jewish benediction: First, the God Who is praised is *my* God, for I speak to Him, in intimate, personal address—directly, without mediation or personification. Second, the God Who is addressed is *our* God, the one God known by the Jewish people, who "discovered" Him, and who have maintained a very special relationship to Him, ever since. Third, this God—Who merits "my" praise, and deserves "our" gratitude—is the God of the whole world, Creator of heaven and earth, worthy to be worshipped by all men, *in the ways known unto them.*

Thus, in Judaism, God is *personalized* without being *personified;* man speaks as an "I" to a God Who is intimately known as "Thou," to paraphrase Martin Buber. Is this not what the Psalmist had already said, centuries before: "The Lord is nigh unto all them that call upon Him."

Thus, too, in Judaism, the Jew calls out to his God, as a member of a people which seeks to be a light unto the nations, by making its God the God of all nations, *without requiring them to convert to Judaism.* Is this not what Micah had already taught, long years ago: "For out of Zion shall go forth the law, and the word of the Lord from Jerusalem . . . *For let all the peoples walk each one in the name of its god, but we will walk in the name of the Lord our God for ever and ever.*"

# XVII Of Jews and Non-Jews

Most modern rabbis, at some time or another, have been asked this question by inquiring people outside of their faith: "If Judaism is so insistently a monotheistic faith, with so universal a point of view, why does it not, like Christianity and Islam, actively engage in missionizing the world? How is it that one does not meet up with 'Jewish missionaries' in search of converts?"

The answer to this question has already, in part, been given. The fact that Judaism will accept but not seek converts is due, to some extent, to the historical record. During the Roman period, when Jews were competing with Christians for new converts among the pagans, many of the hard-won proselytes continued to pine for the old ways and sought to incorporate their heathen practices into their new "Jewish" religion. We have noted the negative reaction of the ancient rabbis to this withering-away and watering-down of strict monotheistic practices.

But there is really a deeper theological reason for this situation—one that far outweighs the historical causes. Occasionally, in modern times, groups of Jews have attempted to support and to justify the universalism of Judaism by organizing associations to foster the spread of public information about Judaism—thus to assist and encourage all those outside of Judaism who might be interested or curious to consider the possibility of conversion. For it is a strange condition to be in, difficult for most people to grasp: How can you be willing to accept converts, the sincere questioner demands of Jews, and yet not vigorously pursue your mission. Quite honestly, he asks: Either you believe in your mission, or you do not; either you proselytize or you do not!

Normative Judaism has responded to this challenge without being forced into the fixed and frozen position of "either-or." And the answer stems from the very core of the Jewish outlook upon the world. Universalism, Judaism insists, does not demand a monolithic, totalitarian religious viewpoint, nor does a universal God require or depend upon a universal church in which He is worshipped. Deeply ingrained in the Tradition is the belief that any good man, Jew or non-Jew, may be acceptable in the sight of the Lord. This is the key to Jewish reticence on the subject of missionizing. Because its philosophy of God and man does not rest upon the belief that through Judaism—and Judaism alone—can people be saved from eternal doom and damnation, it lacks the enkindled passion necessary to spark a drive to Judaize the world. Judaism possesses a universal view, but a kind different from the one the Moslems or Christians have understood.

The Jewish view, already accepted in the Talmudic age, and reasserted by Maimonides, most-respected medieval Jewish theological authority, is summed up in the dictum: "The righteous men among all the peoples of the world have a share in the World to Come." While the rabbis required Jews to fulfill the 613 Commandments of the Pentateuch, non-Jews, in their view, could be adjudged righteous if they observed but *seven* of these commandments. The "Seven Commandments required of the sons of Noah," as this special "Torah" for the non-Jew came to be known, were considered to be the basic rules of morality which were binding upon all mankind. All men were commanded to refrain from (1) idolatry; (2) incest and adultery; (3) bloodshed; (4) blasphemy; (5) injustice and lawlessness; (6) robbery; and (7) inhumane conduct, such as the eating of the flesh of a living animal.

A Jew believes that as a Jew he must fulfill the Law and its commandments—this is the obligation of the "sons of the Covenant," and it is binding upon all the generations of Israel. It is in this sense that he considers himself a member of the "chosen people." For this reason, every time he is honored in the synagogue by being called up to the reading of the Torah lesson, he pronounces this special benediction: "Praised be Thou, O Lord our God, King of the Universe, Who hast chosen us from amongst all the people *by* requiring that we fulfill the laws of the Torah . . ." The special place

which Jews have claimed for themselves in the divine economy has given rise to all kinds of misunderstandings. They
have been accused of religious chauvinism, of tribal exclu-
sivism, and of arrogant national pride. But the Jewish doctrine of the "chosenness of Israel" imputes no inferiority to
those who are outside of Israel; on the contrary, the non-Jew
has fewer spiritual obligations, less strenuous moral commit-
ments, because he has not been given a Torah to fulfill.
Those who have refused to understand this Jewish concept
have agreed with the modern epigram:

> How odd
> Of God
> To Choose
> The Jews!

But the counter-epigram serves as a summary of the way in
which Judaism understands the matter:

> It's not
> So odd.
> The Jews
> Chose God!

Indeed, history is a testimony to the fact that the Jews were
the first to choose God by dedicating their collective destiny
to the covenant made at Sinai, when Israel agreed to live
by the Torah. That covenant is reciprocal, two-sided; it is a
bilateral contract, in which Israel has undertaken to do the
will of God, but not for the sake of special privilege. On the
contrary, the covenant imposes special hardships, and often
involves the whole people in pain, suffering, even threats of
extinction.

To what end, then, the suffering? Of what spiritual value,
the covenant? The answers to these questions confront us
squarely with the way in which Judaism has understood its
universal mission. Nor are they the finely-spun arguments
of theologians or philosophers, with which they attempt to

read their personal beliefs into history. *Isaiah* spelled out the answers:

> I the Lord have called thee in righteousness,
> And have taken hold of thy hand,
> And kept thee, and set thee for a covenant of the people,
> For a light of the nations;
> To open the blind eyes,
> To bring out the prisoners from the dungeon
> And them that sit in darkness out of the prison house.
>
> (Isa. 42:6–7)

The mission of a Torah-covenanted people is no mere parochialism, nor is it related to the ethnic or religious survival of Jews alone. "A light of the nations"—this is its blazing beacon, and its purpose to bring the nations of the world closer to the one God, that they may learn the ways of peace and justice, thus to serve the one Maker of all men. This is why Judaism can steadfastly maintain its belief that righteous men among all the peoples "have a share in the World to Come"— and need not be converted to Judaism in order to justify their lives. And this is also why Judaism continues to project its very insistent and unique presence, without seeking "to convert men to Judaism, in order that they be saved." Those who desire to cast in their lot with the people of Israel, out of sincere and sober conviction, are welcomed; but to seek or hunt for them would imply that so long as they are not Jews, they are considered to be inferior in the sight of the Lord. For modern Judaism can emulate the feelings of many Jewish teachers, who, although they lived in the intolerant Middle Ages, faithfully regarded both Christianity and Islam as precious instruments of the divine will. Said Maimonides: "All these teachings of Jesus the Nazarene and the Ishmaelite (Mohammed) who arose after him were intended . . . to prepare the whole world to worship God together as one." Indeed, in the Jewish view, the world —not to exclude Christendom and Islam—requires the continued and creative existence of both daughter religions.

It is this special brand of religious universalism by which Christianity and the western world need to be confronted. Christianity, in its pristine days, when it was still a "sect" of Judaism, emerged as a unifying force in a world which was decaying for lack of a centrifugal, trans-national force. The early Christians criticized the Jewish Pharisees for they deemed them to be too separatist, too self-concerned, too parochial in clinging to the doctrine of the divine election of Israel as the chosen people. When Paul taught that in Christ there is neither Jew nor Gentile, Greek nor barbarian, he was addressing himself specifically to what he thought was the ethnocentric provincialism of the Jewish community in the view it held regarding its own chosenness.

But a crucial paradox developed. Whereas Christianity rejected Israel's special relationship to God as producing too narrow a world-view, it substituted itself as the new Israel— the elect of God, and proceeded to deify its church as the *mystical body of Christ*. While the Pharisees may not have been especially interested in the religious fate of the heathen nations—and this remained a scandal to Christianity which was intent upon universalizing its mission—these Jewish teachers never debarred the *righteous* non-Jew from sharing in the salvation that was the reward of righteousness.

Christian universalism, however, had made no place for the non-Christian in its esoteric scheme of things to be. The Roman Church insisted that Christ is God and that the Church is Christ. Orthodox Protestants had not gone much beyond this, substituting for this doctrine the affirmation of its faith in "the universal priesthood of believers." For devout Christians, faith in Jesus as the Christ was the only valid belief—at least until recently.

This is why Christianity—and the world beyond it—needs to be reminded of Judaism's dialogue with it. For Judaism still insists—and by its continued corporate existence persistently maintains—that while God is one, His children are many, and the proper universal task of each is to live by His teaching, leaving final judgments only to Him.

No people is essentially wayward, and furthermore, mere mutual toleration of each other's errors cannot be the final approach to truth: only when we validate as the divine, the separate roads which lead to the divine, can there develop the true love of each other—which, after all, is the ultimate concern, the final and consummate goal of a common humanity.

James Parkes, wise student of Judaism and Christianity, himself an Anglican clergyman has aptly and pithily summarized this need: "Judaism is a way of life, and it converts by communicating some part of its way of life to the nations among which and within which it lives. Because of this . . . the world, so to say, notices when a Jew becomes a Christian; and the convert must cease to be a Jew. But it does not notice when Jewish influence affects the political and social life of a Christian community, and the community itself does not notice that it has been in some respects converted to Judaism."

This explains why most Christians have little awareness of the question, and only when "famous" people convert to Judaism do they realize that this religion, like their own, is also a conversionary faith.

Yet, be it remembered: Judaism does not seek *converts*! It seeks to convert the peoples of the world to the higher implications of their monotheistic faiths. Jews believe that this may happen, not so much by making others into Jews, as by making themselves into better people.

## The Messiah: Why Jews Rarely Convert

All of this may help to explain why, despite the efforts of centuries-long endeavor on the part of Christians and Moslems, Jews have rarely converted to these other religions.

When there is decisive competition between two rival and contending missionary faiths, invariably one will hold sway over the other. When this takes place, the air is charged with a dramatic feeling of "either-or." Indeed, such was the case in the first centuries of the Christian Era, when both Judaism and Christianity were vying for converts. Many of the early Christian Church Councils dealt with the problem of "Judaizing" practices within the Church, seeking to root these out because of their desire to make certain that prospective converts made no mistake about the *Christian* character of the Church. Obviously, there was fear that in some ways the zeal of a missionary Judaism might capture the heart, if not the body, of the Church. Similarly, the rabbis of this period made every effort possible to steer clear of rituals which might in some way be construed to be overly similar to those current in Christianity. In the first centuries of the Common Era, as Jewish and Christian missionaries dramatically competed with each other, the traffic between the two communities was relatively heavy: Jews were converting to Christianity, Christians to Judaism, and pagans to one or the other.

But once Jews reworked their concept of the mission, and no longer actively engaged in proselytizing, the situation changed radically. If Jews had remained interested in winning Christians over to Judaism—as Christians are still interested in "saving" Jews—it is conceivable that in such a spirited contest many Jews might fall away from Judaism and accept Christianity. One important reason why many sincere Christians still find it difficult to understand why Jews do not accept Christianity in greater numbers, is linked up with the Jewish concept of universalism. Since Jews believe that in all monotheistic faiths the one God is worshipped, if ethical behavior is the end-product, they do not see Christianity as a rival, and thus are not attracted to it by the magnetism which rivalry often creates. Christianity can survive, and at its side Judaism may grow and create—and Jews see in this situation, not the curse, but the blessing of God. For Jews, both in their practice of Judaism, and in their world-view, have never equated unity with uniformity. Unity is based upon a recognition of the existence of vital differences among men who can nevertheless cooperate through acts of mutual understanding and helpfulness. Uniformity, on the other hand, stifles and retards the development of creative relationships because it desires to obliterate rather than to recognize differences.

Much of the hate in the world has been, sadly, the result of strong religious rivalries—all in the name of God. Here again, is another reason why most Jews—excepting possibly those who are unwilling or unable to withstand the social pressures which are the lot of a member of a minority—have not found it necessary or seemly to accept Christianity. Essentially, to do so would mean that they would be giving up their own brand of ethical universalism in exchange for Christian universalism which requires uniformity as regards faith in its Messiah.

One might say, as some have said, that the Jews, who have given the world the concept of Messiah, surely need not hold out stubbornly to the Christian world, claiming that the Messiah has not yet come. Instinctively, however, Jews have distrusted all would-be claimants to messiahship. Surely, as far as they are concerned, the "Messianic Age" which Christians claimed to have arrived with the coming of Jesus, has not brought peace to the people of Israel. Far from it: Jews have suffered at the hands of some devout Christians in the past—men who rationalized their unethical behavior toward Jews by loading upon their victims the divine blame for not accepting Jesus. This kind of "religious" thinking surely could not succeed in drawing Jews closer to Christianity.

But even had the history of Christianity been less marred by some of the blind hate of religious zealots—even if Judaism had had as uneventful a relationship with Christianity as, say, Buddhism—Jews would still find it difficult to accept the idea of the Christian Messiah. There are at least three reasons for this:

While Jews contributed the idea of Messiah to the treasury of world thought, and while Judaism still holds onto its original significance, Jews, somehow, have sensed that as an ideal it was inspiring, but as an actuality, it has been quite unfulfilling. Many men besides Jesus had proclaimed themselves as the Jewish Messiah. The moment, however, that they also claimed to possess supernatural powers and boasted of special kinship to divinity, they were rejected by their strongly monotheistic people, and could no longer be contained within the community and the faith of Israel. Thus, even those Jews who have strayed far from their religious heritage, and do not faithfully observe Jewish law, are instinctively on their guard against the possibilities of personifying a God in the name of Messiah. Some Jews may adhere to the Law in less strict fashion than their forefathers, but as Jews they are monotheists in no less strict a construction.

Orthodox Jews, of course, believe in the coming of a Messiah, but only in the form of a man—not a God—who will serve as the "anointed one"—the king of Israel—to lead his people as the "light of the nations." The Messiah, they believe, will not come until Israel is restored to its place as the Messiah-people, to become a moral example to the world of the teachings of the Lord. *Until the Messiah comes, Jews surely must remain Jews!* Indeed, they contend, he will not come until all Jews become better Jews—until they scrupulously observe the Law, thus becoming worthy of their special role as the teachers of the nations.

Conservative and Reform Jews, most of whom do not accept the idea of a personal Messiah, surely can not be expected to accept the Christian Messiah. These Jews speak of a "Messianic Age" yet to come; indeed, they would say that, in essence, the Jewish Messiah idea never centered upon the personality of the man—he was but a symbol—but rather would be experienced in the "Days of the Messiah." The special role of Jewish Messianism—that which sets Judaism apart, and makes its viewpoint distinctive—is the forward-thrust of its ethical optimism. Most peoples have spoken of a Golden Age in the past tense; Jews, alone, believe in a Golden Age, yet to be—not outside of history, but within it! While these Conservative and Reform Jews no longer personalize the Messiah—perhaps because they fear that such an envisagement might lead to a modern idolatry—they are impelled religiously by the hope for the improvement of mankind, and the ultimate achievement of the Good Society—the Kingdom of God on earth. This Kingdom of God, they have equated with the Messianic Age, and warlessness is its chief hallmark.

In the earliest days of Christian history, Christians and Jews differed with each other principally in regard to the Messiah—and that difference was primarily a chronological, not a theological one. Jews believed that the Messiah was still to come; Christians proclaimed that he had already come. In time, however, a much more radical difference developed as Christianity moved further away from its Jewish origins. The meaning of Messiah—not only his advent—was changed. Thus, the name Christianity came to signify a very novel interpretation of the old Hebrew word Messiah. The new idea is defined, among others, by John, who refers to the age of the Messiah as "a kingdom *not* of this world" (John 18:36). But Jews always understood, and understand still, that the Messianic world is God's world and that God's world—exalted and idealized—can be found in *this world*. Thus Judaism never became a world-weary religion, and could never despair of man's ethical possibilities; its Messiah-idea indeed, is intimately linked to a belief in man's spiritual potential—not to his spiritual failure. Even the Orthodox Jew who persists in personalizing the Messiah, still sees him only as "a righteous man ruling in the fear of God"—his function being to help bring ethical perfection to the world. The progress of humanity, however, does not depend upon him but upon humanity, itself. In the long run, and in this world, God is going to be the winner, because man, whom He created, will learn to repent of his *evil ways* and do *good works*.

Christian preoccupation with sin is still another barrier to Jewish acceptance of Christianity. This insistence that man is a sinner, merely because he was born a man, seems to Jews to indicate a moral pessimism which is not in consonance with their way of thinking. Modern Christian teachers make much of a "crisis theology." Many of those who are "returning to religion" have been attracted by this mysterious leap of faith which helps to overcome anxiety about man's frailty, creatureliness and finitude. But Jews, because of the background of their own world-views, seem to sense that this "new" theology is not new at all; it has a familiar ring to it. It is, for them, but a modern restatement of what has been a perennial Christian obsession with man's death and earthly mortality. But how does one hurdle these obstacles, Christian theologians ask, if not through faith in Jesus? Christian faith eliminates the crisis by offering eternal bliss in the hereafter. Believe in Jesus and destroy death; believe in him not, and be consigned to eternal damnation!

This threat of doom and damnation has been hurled at Jews throughout all of the Christian centuries, ever since their synagogue was labeled by some as the "Synagogue of Satan." Yet, in these very periods, Jews experienced some of their greatest moments of spiritual creativity. The "Dark Ages" never reached them. Their rabbis, scholars, and philosophers continued to develop and heighten their intellectual, scientific, and religious traditions, while most of Europe remained in the thralldom of ignorance and superstition.

This ceaseless spiritual energy may not be unrelated to still another fundamental barrier to Jewish conversion. Jews do recognize "crisis" in their world-view, but not the crisis created by the forbidding face of death. The crisis which Jews understand is the crisis which results from an *unfulfilled life*. This is what motivates the Jew to seek ethical solutions rather than to leap away from life in the name of faith. Why, Jews ask, create additional anxieties by constantly confronting man with the burden of Original Sin and the mystery of the unfathomable world to come? In the words of Dr. Abba Hillel Silver, Jews prefer to train their efforts upon men's "needless and profligate waste of their limited years, the unassayed tasks, the locked opportunities, the talents withering in disuse, and all the summoning but untrodden ways of mind and soul which give rise to men's spiritual malaise and the deep-rooted and undefined sorrows of their lives. . . . Whatever is inherent, universal and inevitable in the race of man does not constitute a crisis."

The crisis of our time, and of all time, Jews say, is essentially moral and not theological. Thus, Jews have no urgent need to convert to a point of view, which, in their judgment, does not offer them better answers to the problems of human life than those they already possess. For the monotheism of the Jew is *ethical* monotheism, and all stress has been placed upon good works as the index of a man's faith.

All Jews who wish to remain Jews, can say together: Not until nations and communities learn to live together in peace, respecting their separate integrities—which, after all, create their differences—can the Messiah or his age, be said to have come.

Jews, then, together with all men of understanding and good will still await the day not yet at hand. Jews must await it, as Jews; Christians, as Christians—that day of which Isaiah sang and dreamed:

> And He shall judge between the nations,
> And shall decide for many peoples;
> And they shall beat their swords into plowshares,
> And their spears into pruning-hooks;
> Nation shall not lift up sword against nation,
> Neither shall they learn war any more.

# XVIII The New Ecumenism:
## From "Interfaith" to Religious Dialogue

For all its blights and sorrows, its wars and hostilities, the twentieth century has also won some important religious credits for itself. Despite many unresolved conflicts and the menacing superpower rivalry, this may yet become known as "The Century of Religious Dialogue."

It is a crucial fact that until recently the great religions have sought to address the whole world, yet they barely spoke *to each other*—certainly not as partners in joint search of elusive truths. Now, within Christendom new winds are blowing. The four-hundred-year-old "cold war" between Catholics and Protestants is yielding to an era of good feeling. The new encounters between the two former adversaries are powered by novel theological drives expressed in terms of an excitingly different spiritual vocabulary: dialogue not disputation, eschatology not conversion. Protestantism, it is now said, needs Catholicism, and Catholicism benefits from Protestantism. Both announce to the world that each will enjoy a fuller appreciation of its own faith because of the creative existence of the other.

The late Father Gustave Weigel, S.J. reminded both groups never to forget that they

> are here as a matter of massive fact, and neither wants to become the other. The goal, therefore, will not be that they do become one church, though this is not a negation of the hope that at some day by God's grace they will. The purpose of the continuous symposium would be to eliminate or reduce the hostilities but not the differences between the two parties. As a result, they could live in peace and security without the constant fear of raids and inroads. The Catholic would in Christian love respect the Protestant, not simply as another man but as a Protestant. The Protestant would return

this same affection. This is not church union; it is neighborliness of love and Christian charity.

All of which adds up to a new and radical view of Christian unity. The ultimate hope of Christendom, "that all may be one," is deferred to God and His saving power. Some day, yes, in God's good time. But how shall Protestants and Catholics face each other now?

Dr. Robert McAfee Brown, a leading Protestant theologian, suggested:

As a step toward that time when in ways beyond our present knowing, by the mysterious workings of the Holy Spirit, we are drawn closer together than we are now, it is appropriate that we acknowledge that the existence of each group can be a source of ministry to the other and that as we are most characteristically and creatively ourselves, we shall have the most to contribute to one another's enrichment.

In this spirit Christian leaders no longer appear as rivals seeking to overwhelm their opponents in theological battle. Their older suspicion and distrust, which had built high walls of human separation, are beginning to yield to earnest desires and energetic efforts to understand and respect their differing doctrines and traditions. Even those Protestant and Catholic leaders who are not ready to sign an immediate peace treaty leading to early reunion seem quite prepared to think in terms of armistice and coexistence.

Can this revolutionary turn in the history of Catholic-Protestant relations transcend its self-erected bounds and have a moral effect on the total religious climate of our communities? Clearly, Christian ecumenism is one of the century's most hopeful -isms. Many other -isms, however, starting as if they had all of mankind sincerely at heart, ended ingloriously only self-concerned, protecting their own institutions, guarding their own boundaries. Will

Christian ecumensim serve all the world or just its own church?

Catholic-Protestant ecumenism surely serves the Churches. It is designed to help Christian partners to the dialogue live in charity until the day that all Christians regard as their ultimate fulfillment—when "all may be one," and the scourge of Christian disunity is eradicated. But now should the Jew react to Christian ecumenism and its possible consequences? Does "Christian unity" resolve old problems, or does it pose new ones for him? What religious response could he make to those new ecumenists if their search for Christian unity were also to be extended to him? Had he not better work in concert with Christians as citizens only in the secular-social arena rather than seek to foster a religious unity that cannot really be intended for him as a Jew?

No doubt, the ecumenical movement raises new problems for Jews, problems that mercifully had been left dormant during the earlier period of interfaith activities. Jews had felt relatively safe participating in the social rituals created by the religion of Interfaith wherein all religions were accorded coequal status, precisely because the civil religion of democracy believes in none of them separately, but only in all of them together.

In this new age of Christian ecumenism Jews are now invited to participate in interfaith activity *from the ground of faith,* and to participate in the dialogue that has begun between Catholics and Protestants. As a result, Jews are now regarded also as important religious partners. Yet to become full and equal participants in this effort raises paradoxical questions for both Christians and Jews.

A word, first, about Jewish reticence. It is, of course, well grounded in many earlier experiences, a holdover from the tragic Jewish history. After the fifth century, when Christianity became the state religion of the Roman Empire, the classical rabbinic desire to teach the world and

[163]

to reach out for sincere proselytes was cast aside.* And in the ghettos of Europe it would be unnatural—not to say impossible—for them to establish spiritual or intellectual contacts with the Christian world. Any such efforts were nothing more than rigged polemical debates—not even-handed dialogues—set up by an all-powerful Church intent on proving Judaism's inferiority to Christianity. They usually culminated either in the burning of Jewish books, repressive ordinances, or even outright expulsion of Jews. True, the royal family of Adiabene, a province of Parthia, had converted to Judaism in the first century of the Christian era and its queen, Helena, spent many years in Jerusalem. (Her body was later brought there, to be buried in a tomb that is still standing.) In the fifth century, the kings of Himyar in southern Arabia adopted Judaism, and in the first half of the eighth century the upper classes of the Khazars in the Volga-Caucasus region—they were of Turkic stock—had also converted. Still, as the eminent poet-philosopher Rabbi Judah Ha-Levi of Spain, wrote in the twelfth century:

> When Christians and Muslims fight, Jews—who are in the middle—are made to suffer, too. Would they not also be hurt even if irenic discussions between unequals would replace disputation?

Jews came to fear dialogue as much as debate, since they were still not regarded as religious partners.

What if twentieth-century Christians were to learn to see Jews and come to regard Judaism not as a surpassed community of belief, but as both a living force and a vital

---

*See Matthew 23:15. The author claims that Pharisees will "traverse sea and land to make a single proselyte." This suggestion of an active and vigorous proselytization among the Talmudic rabbis may be an exaggeration. Yet, the prideful references of the Talmud to such luminaries as Rabbi Meir, Rabbi Akiba, Shemaya, and Avtalyon—tracing their origin to proselytes to Judaism—leaves no doubt that the authors of the Talmud were not averse to "recruiting" still others like them. See also the excellent chapter, "Conversion of Gentiles" in George F. Moore, *Judaism* (Vol. 1), Harvard University Press, 1932, pp. 323–353.

partner-in-faith? Would Jews then find it possible to enter into serious religious dialogue with these new ecumenical Christians?

Much would depend on the answers Christian leaders were to give to several key religious issues still remaining at the heart of the great Christian-Jewish divide.

Indeed, as the twentieth century moves to its close, there are encouraging signs that the Christian world is moving toward the resolution of many of the unresolved *religious* issues that have stood in the way of true dialogue for almost two millenia. As recently as the 1930s and 1940s, the Churches, with only few notable exceptions, were content to remain officially silent while six million European Jews were wantonly slaughtered for no reason other than that they were Jews. Hitler's final solution to the Jewish problem—his diabolical plan to erase them from the face of the earth—brought forth no serious religious protest from most Christian leaders and their followers. That silence of the Church during those cataclysmic days would, ironically, become the spiritual springboard for a new ecumenism—a new heart and a new spirit—that began to emerge within Christendom shortly after Pope John XXIII convened the historic Second Vatican Council in the early 1960s.

What was the religious picture like in America before that time? It was only in 1928 that the National Conference of Christians and Jews was organized. (A few years later a similar organization was formed in Canada, the Canadian Council of Christians and Jews.) It entered upon the scene only after many Catholics and Protestants came to realize that the vicious, hysterical waves of anti-Catholicism then sweeping the country threatened to destroy the very fabric of democracy. Prominent rabbis, ministers, and priests banded together nationally with but one clear goal: *not to enter into religious discussions, but, on the contrary, to avoid them.* Their purpose was to take the issue of religion out of the arena of politics and social

warfare and to concentrate instead on helping to make
American democracy work. Their efforts were almost entirely dedicated to combating the religious bigotry that had
sought to turn one group of American citizens against the
other.

For many years thereafter interfaith activity in America was expressed primarily in civic symbols: "tolerance," "brotherhood," and the "American way," were
its basic catchwords. A "tolerance trio" consisting of a
prominent rabbi, a Presbyterian minister, and a Catholic
priest toured the country, speaking before business and
community groups in what resembled a Rotary Club
goodwill performance. "Brotherhood Week," set between Lincoln's and Washington's Birthdays, was established as a new annual American commemoration.
Although ostensibly under religious auspices, it became a
novel ritual of the national, secular, "civil religion."

It would take the full impact of the Holocaust—the an-
nihilation of six million—as well as a revolutionary effort
on the part of the Holy Father himself, Pope John XXIII,
to come to grips with the "teaching of contempt" for Jews
and Judaism, which had been part of Christian thought for
almost nineteen hundred years, before secular interfaith
activities could be transformed into attempts to establish
true religious dialogue between Christians and Jews.*

Christians had first to be reminded at the highest levels
that the Church condemns anti-Semitism at any time and
by anyone. That could come about only when the Church
was ready to reexamine its own Jewish origin, its roots in
the mother faith.

In his search for "church renewal"—*aggiornio-
mento*—Pope John XXIII convened the Second Vatican

*For a significant discussion concerning Pope John's reaction to this question
see Jules Isaac, *The Teaching of Contempt: Christian Roots of Anti-Semitism*,
McGraw Hill Paperbacks, New York, 1963—especially the biographical intro-
duction by Claire Huchet Bishop which describes Isaac's historic audience with
the Pope in 1960 concerning the theme of his book.

Council in 1962. It could not then have been foreseen that this "new ecumenism" of Catholics would ultimately stretch beyond their fellow Christians, the Protestants, and embrace the Jews as well. Yet, by 1965 the Vatican had issued a landmark decree, known as *"Nostra Aetate Number 4,"* or, called more popularly, *The Jewish Declaration.* The document asserted that not only had the Church received the Hebrew Bible from the Jews but that it *still draws sustenance from Judaism,* "the well-cultivated olive tree on to which have been grafted the wild shoots, the Gentiles." It was a bold attempt to wipe away the dark chapters of almost two thousand years of Church-sponsored anti-Jewishness. The Church proclaimed that the Jewish religion possessed continuing validity, for the covenant God had made with the Jewish people had never been annulled: "He does not repent of the gifts he makes or of the calls He issues." Further, the *Declaration* took pains to emphasize the Jewishness of Christianity itself. Brotherly dialogues with Jews soon became the order of the day, especially in the American branch of the Roman Catholic Church. To help foster these efforts, the American Catholic Bishops' Secretariat for Catholic-Jewish Relations was established in 1967. A goodly number of area bishops also created their own diocesan commissions in order to implement the dialogue called for by the *Declaration.*

Then in 1975 the newly established Vatican Commission for Religious Relations with the Jews issued its own "Guidelines and Suggestions for Implementing the Conciliar Declaration *Nostra Aetate, Number 4.*" These guidelines attempted to fill in certain notable voids that had been overlooked or glossed over in the earlier *Jewish Declaration.* More particularly, they dealt with questions concerning the relationship of Jews and Judaism to the State of Israel as well as sensitive areas touching on Christian proselytization of Jews. That same year, the

American bishops picked up the thread of these Vatican guidelines and issued their own "Statement on the Jews." Concerning Israel they noted that "an overwhelming majority of Jews see themselves bound in one way or another to the land of Israel. Most Jews see this tie to the land as essential to their Jewishness. Whatever difficulties Christians may experience in sharing this view, they should strive to understand this link between land and people." And on proselytizing, they applauded the Vatican guidelines: "Dialogue demands respect for the other as he is; above all, respect for his faith and his religious convictions." The American prelates explicitly disapproved of all efforts on the part of Catholics to convert Jews.

When these and similar Christian affirmations of Judaism's uninterrupted vitality and integrity were pronounced—not only by Catholics but also by many Protestants, as we shall see—Jewish religious leaders began to regard the new ecumenical outreach and the fraternal dialogues with less fear and trembling. Traditionally, the outstretched hand had always been offered them only by Christian proselytizers bent on converting them to the "one, true religion"—theirs, and theirs alone. But Catholics, and large numbers of Protestant churches of the nonfundamentalist variety, have now begun to proclaim their willingness to accept Judaism as a living, coequal religion and are dropping their millenial desire to convert Jews to Christianity as the price for fraternal, religious coexistence. In these new circumstances, many Jews have also become more forthcoming and welcome the new opportunity to speak to Christians about matters of faith as partners-in-dialogue.

The ongoing efforts of the Roman Catholic Church to continue in the spirit of Vatican II's *Jewish Declaration* have indeed been received warmly by most Jewish leaders in America. Yet some important stumbling blocks remain on the path leading to a fuller understanding. They center around the problem of the State of Israel as it is often regarded in liberal Protestant circles, as well as the continuing missionary hope about the Jews that many evangelical fundamentalist Christians still harbor.

Problems caused by the negative image of Jews and Judaism still found in some Christian religious textbooks—especially those intended for unsuspecting Sunday School children—remain a matter of serious concern to those who desire to promote and enhance sincere Christian-Jewish dialogue.

Wittingly or not, the mainline liberal Protestant churches, as symbolized in their nationwide umbrella organization the National Council of Churches, often helped to impede Christian-Jewish dialogue. Not content with its apathetic, quiescent attitude in June 1967 before and during the Six-Day War, when Israelis were threatened with the possibility of catastrophic defeat, the National Council of Churches continued to side politically with the Arab states and to disregard Israel's need for security surrounded as it is by Arab countries holding, except for Egypt, to a "no-recognition, no-negotiation" stance.

An astute Protestant scholar, Franklin H. Littell, has pithily summarized the problem Jews may continue to experience with these liberal Christian groups: "The thing the nineteenth-century liberal Protestant, the Christian humanitarian, cannot grasp is the Jew who is a winner, a citizen soldier of liberty and dignity, who does not have to beg protection of a patron or toleration of a so-called Christian nation . . . This is precisely the reason why Israel is a stone of stumbling and why also the generally covert anti-Semitism of liberal Protestantism can be just as dangerous as the overt anti-Semitism of the radical right."

On the other hand, the rise of "born-again" Christianity in America and the growth of militant, right-wing evangelical cadres fostered by television preachers also threaten sound Christian-Jewish relations. Under a variety of names these groups often speak as one with a strident, patriotic voice, as "Christian America." Essentially, they are the self-same old fundamentalist Christians who now, making active use of television, have made the whole country into their potential Bible Belt. Whether called the Moral Majority or other names, they are seeking to politicize Christianity by calling into action those dormant WASP forces that feel threatened by pluralism and the multiple life choices offered by the new ethnicity in America. These groups may speak out in behalf of the State of Israel as "concerned Christians" who reject the frequent pro-Arab pronouncements of their avowed adversaries, the liberal Protestant churches. Yet, sensitive Jews are not unaware of the fact that these evangelicals are also essentially triumphalist Christians whose "Christian Zionism" cannot conceal their hope that Israel will fade away with the second coming of Jesus as the acknowledged Messiah of the Jews as well as of the world. Nor do many of these neofundamentalists take the liberating step of renouncing the validity of the Christian mission to the Jews. The conversion of the Jews remains an integral part of the theological position of most evangelical churches.

In a highly sensitive area, the religious classrooms of the church Sunday School, where many of the earliest impressions of Christian teaching are often indelibly imprinted, much damage has also been done to Jewish-Christian relations. The results of a 1960 study conducted at Yale University on Protestant attitudes toward Judaism and Jews, as reflected in standard textbook material used by the various denominations, elicited this comment from Reinhold Niebuhr, the eminent theologian: "The evidence of the study has convinced me that the religious and racial sources of anti-Semitism are at least equal, and perhaps the religious source may be the more powerful."

And his colleague, then Dean of the faculty at Union Theological Seminar, New York, Dr. John C. Bennett, agreed, noting that Christian teaching in many contemporary church textbooks in America "does contain elements which stimulate anti-Jewish prejudice." Dr. Bernhard E. Olson, who conducted the study at Yale, also noted the difficulties:

> It is as impossible . . . for a Christian teacher to communicate the Christian message without reference to Judaism as it would be to teach American history without referring to England and the founding fathers. . . .
>
> This inevitable Hebrew involvement in religious instruction makes the Jew something more than just another minority which happens to get mentioned in Christian teaching. While a lesson writer might disregard the Negro, unless the outline guide specifies otherwise, he cannot ignore the Jew. . . .
>
> . . . While nothing essentially invidious . . . inheres in the marked prominence of the Jew in Protestant texts, there is in it an ever-present danger. As a minority which inescapably figures in the foreground of Christian thought—and remains an accessible minority in a society which contains deep strains of anti-Semitism—the Jewish community easily becomes a vulnerable target. . . .

Dr. Olson's Yale study broke new ground and helped to establish the need for textbook revision of Christian teaching concerning the Jews. Books on Judaism published since that study are somewhat improved in this area. Yet research conducted in both Protestant and Catholic schools later revealed that their textbooks still contained a great number of references to Jews with some of the vilest comments made about any religious group. The charge of deicide is still frequent, the Jewish covenant is often declared to be ended, and the Pharisees are on many occasions described as subhuman. Clearly, the method of teaching Christianity in its relationship to Judaism must constantly be reviewed by Christians if they are to achieve the desired goal of true dialogue.

Happily, in January 1982, a study unit of the World Council of Churches—with which the liberal Protestant National Council of Churches (in the United States) is affiliated—took a giant step forward in its proposed "Guidelines for Jewish-Christian Dialogue." Meeting in Bali, Indonesia, this select group on "Dialogue with People of Living Faiths and Ideologies" offered new and bold suggestions. It is enough to listen to the language of the group itself to be encouraged about prospects for the future. Here are some of the highlights of their new thinking:

## Preface

The relations between Jews and Christians have unique characteristics because of the ways in which Christianity historically emerged out of Judaism. Christian understandings of that process constitute a necessary part of the dialogue and give urgency to the enterprise. As Christianity came to define its own identity over against Judaism, the church developed its own understandings, definitions, and terms for what it had inherited from Jewish traditions, and for what it read in the Scriptures common to Jews and Christians. In the process of defining its own identity, the Church defined Judaism and assigned to the Jews definite roles in its understanding of God's acts of salvation. It should not be surprising that Jews resent those Christian theologies in which they as a people are assigned to play a negative role. History has demonstrated over and again how short the step is from such patterns of thought in Christianity to overt acts of condescension, persecution and worse. . . .

For those reasons there is special urgency for Christians to listen, through study and dialogue, to ways in which Jews understand their history and their traditions, their faith and their obedience "in their own terms." Furthermore, a mutual listening to how each is perceived by the other may be a step toward overcoming fears and correcting misunderstandings that have thrived in isolation. . . .

## Toward a Christian Understanding of Judaism

. . . In the understanding of many Christians, Judaism as a living tradition came to an end with the coming of Christ and with the destruction of the second temple of Jerusalem; the Church replaced the Jews as God's people, and the Judaism that survived is a fossilized religion of legalism.

In this view the covenant of God with the people of Israel was only a preparation for the coming of Christ—after which it was abrogated. Judaism of the first centuries before and after the birth of Jesus was therefore called "Late Judaism." The Pharisees were considered to represent the acme of legalism, Jews and Jewish groups were portrayed as negative models, and the truth and beauty of Christianity were thought to be enhanced by setting up Judaism as false and ugly.

Through a renewed study of Judaism and in dialogue with Jews, Christians became aware that Judaism in the time of Christ was in an early stage of its long life. Under the leadership of the Pharisees the Jewish people began a spiritual revival of remarkable power which gave them the vitality capable of surviving the catastrophe of the loss of the temple. It gave birth to Rabbinic Judaism which produced the Mishnah and Talmud and built the structures for a strong and creative life through the centuries. . . .

Christians should remember that some of the controversies reported in the New Testament between Jesus and the "scribes and Pharisees" find parallels within Pharisaism itself and its heir, Rabbinic Judaism. These controversies took place in a Jewish context, but when the words of Jesus came to be used by Christians who did not identify with the Jewish people as Jesus did, such sayings often became weapons in anti-Jewish polemics and thereby their original intention was tragically distorted. . . .

Judaism, with its rich history of spiritual life, produced the Talmud as the normative guide for Jewish life in thankful response to the grace of God's covenant with the people of Israel. Over the centuries important commentaries, profound philosophical works and poetry of spiritual depth have been added. For Jews the Talmud is as central and authoritative as the New Testament is for Christians. . . .

### Authentic Christian Witness

Rejection of proselytism and advocacy of respect for the integrity and the identity of all persons and all communities of faith are urgent in relation to Jews, especially those who live as minorities among Christians. Steps toward assuring non-coercive practices are of highest importance. In dialogue ways should be found for the exchange of concerns, perceptions and safeguards in these matters . . .

### Anti-Semitism—A Continuing Concern in the Jewish-Christian Dialogue

Christians must face honestly the tragic history of anti-Semitism, which includes the massacre of Jews in Europe and the Middle East during the Crusades, the Inquisition, pogroms and the Holocaust. It is only by facing this history that Christians can understand the deep-rooted suspicion that many Jews even today have of Christians and Christianity. Christians are called upon to fight anti-Semitism with all the resources at their disposal, the more so since there are disturbing signs of new and increased anti-Semitism in many parts of the world. Those who live in parts of the world where there is a record of anti-Semitic acts are duty bound to unmask for all Christians the ever-present danger they have come to recognize in anti-Judaism and anti-Semitism . . .

One Christian response to the Holocaust must be a resolve that it will never happen again. Teachings of contempt for Jews and Judaism in certain Christian traditions were a spawning ground for the evil of the Nazi Holocaust. The Church must learn so to preach and teach the Gospel as to make sure that it cannot be used against the Jewish people. The Christian churches must be in the forefront of any effort to prevent conditions which might lead to further persecution and another slaughter of the Jewish people. . . .

### The Land

The words from the World Council of Churches Guidelines on Dialogue that one of the functions of dialogue is to allow participants to describe and witness to their faith 'in their own terms' are of particular significance for the understanding of the bond between the Land of Israel and the Jewish people. This bond has, after many centuries of dispersion, found expression in the State of Israel. The need for the State of Israel to exist in security and peace is fundamental to Jewish consciousness and therefore is of paramount importance in any dialogue with Jews. . . .

These proposed guidelines may yet represent a milestone in the history of Protestant-Jewish relations. Even after so many centuries in which postbiblical Judaism was disparagingly dismissed as a "fossil" by both Catholic and Protestant theologians, not only do the Vatican documents on the Jews but now also those of mainline Protestant churches urge their adherents to see in Judaism a vital religion, one with a long and honorable tradition. The centuries-old spirit of rivalry and triumphant superiority seems to have disappeared, and the once pervasive goal in coercing Jews into accepting Christianity is also waning. Furthermore, the Holocaust is no longer glossed over in silence or indifference by Christians as not long ago it was.

Clearly the new ecumenism is a radical departure in the reappraisal of the meaning of Judaism now advocated by Christian leaders. "The fact is," wrote Father John Sheerin, general consultant to the American Bishops' Secretariat for Catholic-Jewish Relations, "the Christian story is a reinterpretation of Israel as the early Christians learned it as Jews. Therefore . . . the dialogue has to be structured by the Jewish frame of reference rather than the Christian."

It is earnestly hoped that "the Jewish frame of reference" offered here will serve all ecumenists—Christians and Jews alike—as a fruitful preface to dialogue, and as a convincing reminder of the eternal bond that links them under the one God of all.

# Glossary

*Amidah:* Literally, the "standing" prayer. This is the basic prayer of all services, and is so named because it is recited standing and in silent devotion.

*Arba Kanfot:* Literally, "four corners" (of a cloak). This is an undergarment with four fringes worn by observant Jews in compliance with Numbers 15:37–41.

*Aron Ha-Kodesh:* The Holy Ark. In this Ark, placed on the east wall of the synagogue are contained the Scrolls of the Law, used for the public reading at services.

*Bar Mitzvah:* Literally, "the son of the commandment." A Jewish boy who has reached the age of thirteen, who is henceforth obligated to fulfill religious duties as an adult.

*Bat Mitzvah:* A new ceremony, for girls of thirteen, which parallels the Bar Mitzvah for the boys.

*Beth Hamidrash:* Literally, "house of study." Study is one of the threefold functions of the synagogue; the other two are prayer and assembly.

*B'nai B'rith:* Literally, "sons of the covenant." Refers to the community of Israel.

*Etrog:* A citron, which, together with the palm branch (lulav), forms the ceremonial cluster used on the Festival of *Sukkot.*

*Gemara:* A Rabbinic code compiled and edited approximately 500 C.E., based upon the earlier code, the Mishnah, and the Bible Law before it.

*Get:* An Aramaic word meaning "bill of divorce."

*Haftarah:* A selected portion from the Prophets of the Hebrew Bible read at the synagogue service after the weekly reading from the Pentateuch.

*Haggadah:* Literally, the "telling of the story." This is the ritual-book which establishes the order of prayers and praises for the home celebration of the Passover festival meal, the *seder.*

*Halakah:* The authorized and normative Law of Jewish religious life, based principally upon the Mosaic Law together with the post-Biblical rabbinic codes and interpretations.

*Hametz:* Leaven. Foods containing leaven or coming in contact with leaven are prohibited to Jews during the Passover holiday. (See Exodus 21:15–20.)

*Hamishah Asar Bi-Shevat:* The fifteenth day of the month of Shevat; celebrated as the "New Year for the Trees."

*Hanukkah:* Literally, "dedication." The Feast of Lights, celebrating the rededication of the Temple by the Maccabees.

*Haroset:* The mixture of nuts, wine, apple and cinammon made to resemble the mortar and the "bricks without straw" which the Israelites made in Egyptian bondage. This symbolical food is eaten at the Passover *Seder* meal.

*Havdalah:* Literally, "separation." The service which concludes the celebration of each Sabbath day, marking a division between the sacred and the profane.

*Hazzan:* The cantor, whose function it is to chant the Hebrew liturgy at the synagogue service.

*Huppah:* A wedding canopy. The celebrants at the wedding service—bride and groom—stand beneath a canopy which serves as a symbol of the home they are about to build.

*Kaddish:* Literally, "sanctification." The doxology recited especially in memory of the departed, by the mourners, at a synagogue service.

*Keriah:* Literally, "rending." The garment of the mourner is torn as a sign of mourning.

*Ketubah:* The religious marriage certificate containing the rights and duties husbands and wives have to each other.

*Kiddush:* Literally, "sanctification." The benediction of praise to God chanted over the cup of wine on Sabbath and festivals, declaring the sanctification of these holy days.

*Kiddushin:* Literally, "sanctification." This is the Hebrew word for the wedding ceremony, implying that the relationship established between man and wife must essentially be a *sacred* one.

*Kohen:* A priest. A descendant of the family of Aaron, who, in Biblical times, were ministers in the ancient Sanctuary.

*Kol Nidre:* Literally, "All vows." This is the opening prayer of the Service on the Eve of Atonement. It has become well known primarily because of the haunting melody with which the words have become associated.

*Kosher:* Food that is ritually acceptable in accordance with Jewish religious practice.

*Levi:* The tribe of Levi, from whom the family of Aaron was descended, acted in ancient times as the assistants to the priests in conducting the divine worship in the ancient Temple.

*Lulav:* The palm branch, together with the myrtle leaves and the willow which form the cluster that is used with the citron at services for the Festival of Sukkot.

*Magen David:* Literally, the "shield of David." Popularly, this refers to the six-pointed star—the Star of David—which is often identified as a denominating symbol of the Jewish people.

*Magrepha:* The name of a musical instrument in the ancient Temple, sometimes supposed to be similar to a water organ.

*Malchut Shamayim:* Literally, the "Kingdom of heaven." It refers to the sovereignty of God in human life.

*Matzah* (plural, *Matzot*): Unleavened cakes of bread used at the Festival of Passover as a symbolical reminder of the "bread of affliction" which Israelites ate at the time of their departure from Egypt.

*Megillah:* Literally, "a scroll." In the Hebrew Bible there are five books which are referred to as *Megillot* (plural). These include the following: the Book of Ecclesiastes, the Book of Esther, the Song of Songs, the Book of Ruth, and the Book of Lamentations.

*Menorah:* A seven-branched candlestick which was part of

the religious symbolism of the ancient Temple, and which
is also found in the modern synagogue.

*Mezzuzah:* A religious symbol placed upon the right doorposts of Jewish homes, containing passages from the Hebrew Bible, intended to remind the occupants of the sanctity of their dwelling.

*Mikvah:* A ritual bath maintained by observant Jews for purification purposes; also used by candidates for conversion
to Judaism, as a ritual for admission.

*Minyan:* Literally, "number." A minyan or quorum of ten
males above the age of thirteen is required for public
Jewish worship. The plural, *minyanim,* is used in the sense
of small congregations of worshippers.

*Mishnah:* A Rabbinic code compiled approximately in the
year 200 C.E. and edited by Rabbi Judah the Prince.

*Mitzvah* (plural, *Mitzvot*): Literally, "a commandment."
The Hebrew Bible consists of 613 *Mitzvot*—divine commandments which are intended to regulate the daily life of
the Jewish people.

*Mohel:* One who performs the rite of circumcision. A mohel
must be qualified by both piety and experience.

*Ner Tamid:* Literally, "eternal light." Above the Holy Ark, in
every synagogue, a perpetual light is kindled to signify the
continuity of faith. The light is never extinguished.

*Parochet:* The covering veil which is placed on the outside of
the Aron Ha-Kodesh.

*Pentateuch:* The Five Books of Moses: Genesis, Exodus,
Leviticus, Numbers, and Deuteronomy.

*Pesach:* Passover. The feast commemorating the exodus from
Egypt. One of the three harvest festivals.

*Purim:* Literally, "lots." The festival whose history is recorded in the Book of Esther.

*Rosh Ha-Kenesset:* The *archisynagogus* or lay head of the
synagogue in the early centuries (C.E.) of its development.

*Rosh Ha-Shanah:* The New Year. This takes place in the Fall
of the year and is commemorated with special services in

the synagogue where the shofar, the ram's horn, is blown to call the congregation to repentance—the theme of the New Year festival.

*Sanhedrin:* Literally, "synod." The ancient council of rabbis which met in Jerusalem, and which had supreme authority in all matters dealing with Jewish law.

*Seder:* Literally, "order of service." The ritual meal conducted in Jewish homes on the first nights of the Passover.

*Shaddai:* Literally, "Almighty." A synonym for God, the word "Shaddai" is placed in the center of a *Mezzuzah* and also forms the symbolism of the phylacteries. *Shaddai,* the Almighty, is thus the everpresent force in each Jewish home and is also recognized as the power which motivates all of life, each day.

*Shavuot:* Literally, "weeks." The Feast of Pentecost or Feast of Weeks. Occurs fifty days (seven weeks) after the second day of Passover.

*Shema:* An abbreviation of the Hebrew prayer, *Shema Yisrael:* Hear, O Israel, the Lord, our God, the Lord is One.

*Shivah:* Literally, "a week." This denotes the period of seven days which mourners are required to observe. They withdraw from their usual pursuits, remaining at home for prayer and meditation immediately following the death of a close kin.

*Shofar:* A ram's horn. This is the instrument which is blown in the synagogue prior to the New Year and on the New Year itself. It is a reminder of the need for repentance and surrender to the will of God.

*Shohet:* One who slaughters animals or fowl according to Jewish ritual. He must be an observant Jew and must be certified by a rabbi as proficient in the knowledge of laws pertaining to slaughter.

*Shul:* A synagogue.

*Siddur:* The order of Service. The compilation of prayers

which has been assembled over the centuries and which comprises the Prayer Book of the Jewish congregation.

*Sidrah* (plural, *Sidrot*): The Biblical "portion of the week." The Five Books of Moses have been divided into fifty-four "portions of the week" which are read in the synagogue throughout the year.

*Simhat Torah:* Literally, the "Rejoicing in the Law." This holiday is celebrated at the close of the Feast of Tabernacles. The annual cycle of Torah reading is concluded and begun again.

*Sukkah:* (plural, *Sukkot*): The *Sukkah* is the hut which Jews erect during the Festival of Booths, and in which they take their meals, whenever possible, during the eight days of the holiday. It is erected to remind the Jew of the primitive and frail abodes in which their ancestors dwelled during their forty years' wandering in the desert of Sinai.

*Sukkot:* The Feast of Tabernacles or Feast of Booths.

*Tallit:* A prayer shawl, worn by males at divine worship in the synagogue.

*Talmud:* The Talmud consists of both Rabbinic codes— Mishnah and Gemara—and forms the basis of Jewish Law compiled by the rabbis in the post-Biblical period.

*Talmud Torah:* An elementary school for Jewish religious education.

*TaNak:* The Hebrew Bible. *TaNak* represents the first letters of *T*orah (Pentateuch), *N*eviim (Prophets) and *K*etuvim (Hagiographa)—the three divisions of Scripture.

*Tephillin:* Phylacteries. These consist of the head-phylactery and the arm-phylactery placed upon the head and arm, which Jewish males over the age of thirteen don for morning prayer, each day—with the exception of Sabbath and Festivals.

*Torah:* In a limited sense the Five Books of Moses (Pentateuch). More broadly, Torah refers to all of Jewish learning and culture, both Biblical and rabbinic.

*Tzitzit:* Literally, "fringes." The Israelites were commanded to make fringes in the corners of their garments. (See Numbers 15:37–41.)

*Viddui:* The "confession" recited by the dying.

*Yahrzeit:* The anniversary of the death of a near relative commemorated by means of special prayers at home and in the synagogue.

*Yetzer Hara:* The "evil inclination" of man's nature.

*Yetzer Ha-tov:* The "good inclination" of man's nature.

*Yizkor:* The memorial service recited by mourners, which forms part of the regular services of the synagogue on four occasions of the year: the Day of Atonement, and the Festivals of *Sukkot,* Passover, and *Shavuot.*

*Yom Kippur:* The Day of Atonement. This occurs ten days following the beginning of the Jewish New Year. It is observed as a solemn day by means of a twenty-four hour fast.

# Index (See page 195 for index to The New Ecumenism.)

Bishops, 18, 19
  Miter of, 50
*B'nai B'rith,* 70
  *See also* Abraham
Book of Common Prayer
  Influenced by Hebrew Psalter, 58
  in the Anglican church, 58
  in the Episcopal church, 58
  in the other Protestant churches, 58
Book of Genesis, 40, 55, 102, 142, 146
Book of Jeremiah, 135, 136
Book of Jonah, 55, 142
Book of Lamentations, 54, 56, 91, 128
Book of Leviticus, 8
Book of Proverbs, 84
Book of Psalms, 25
  orchestra and choir, mentioned in, 47
Books of Moses, Five, 8
"Bridegroom of Genesis," 117
"Bridegroom of the Torah," 117
*B'rit,* 66
  *See also* Circumcision; *Mohel*
Buber, Martin, 133, 148
Buddhist food habits, 86
Buddhist religion, relationship with Judaism, 156


C

Calendar, 99
  Calculation of Christian, 129
  Calculation of Jewish, 129
  Calculation of Moslem, 129
  Civil, in relationship to Jewish, 108
  Easter, date fixed by, 107
  Lunar and solar years, basis of, 102
    discrepancy of days between, 102, 103
  Reformation of, 103
  Regular and leap years of, 104
  Sanhedrin and, 105
Calvinism, 134
Candelabrum, ceremonial, 110, 111
  *See also* Menorah

Cantor, 6, 48
  as minister of music, 25–26
Catholic (*Douay*) Bible, 53
Catholic food habits, 86
  Ash Wednesday and, 86
  Friday "complete abstinence" and, 86
  Holy Communion and, 86
  Holy Saturday and, 86
Chanting of Hebrew Scripture, 44
"Charity box", 110
Chief Rabbi, 32–33
  in England, 32
  in Finland, 33
  in Israel, 33
  in Sweden, 33
"Chosen" People, The, 69, 151, 153
Christ (*See* Jesus)
Christening, derived from Jewish custom, 68
  *See also* Baptism; Circumcision
Christian ceremonies, borrowed from the Rabbis, 30
Christian Church
  credo of, 134
  Hebraic past of, 23
Christian ritual service, 40
Christian services, based on Jewish practices, 15–16
Christian thought, molded by Hebraism, 133
  Hellenism, influence upon, 133
Christianity
  barriers to Jewish acceptance of, 159
  church structure of, 18
  government of the church of, 18
  Jewish influence on symbols of, 37–40
  Judaism compared with, 133–145
  proselytizing, in behalf of, 18
  rivalry for new adherents between Judaism and, 18
Christians, 6
  Jewish interpretation of functions of organized religion, compared with that of, 31
Chronicles (I), 56
Chronicles (II), 56
Church altar cloths, link with Jewish shrouds, 38

*Index*

*tallit,* worn in services of, 51
See also Judaism

## P

Palestine, 4
  academic gatherings in private houses of, 7
  Passover, how observed in, 105, 106
  rabbinical religious courts in, 146
  *tallit* in, 51
Palm Sunday, origin of, 115, 116
Parkes, James, 154
*Parochet,* 36
Passover (*Pesach*), 12, 99, 114, 121, 122–124, 126, 127
  Biblical establishment of, 105
  Jewish religious calendar and, 103
  ritual symbols of, 85, 86
  *Seder* and, 85
  *Song of Songs* on Sabbath, of, 54
*Paternoster,* borrowed from Hebrew tradition, 58
Paul, 17, 126, 127, 138
  Christ, evaluation of, by, 153
Paul V, Pope, 49–50
Pentateuch, 7, 39, 40, 53, 54, 55
  613 Commandments of the, 150
Pentecost (*Shavuot*) 114, 123, 125, 126, 127
  See also Feast of Weeks
Pentecost, *Christian* Feast of, 127
"People of the Book," 47
Perpetual Light (*Ner Tamid*), 36
Persian rule of Second Temple, 3
*Pesach* (*See* Passover)
Pesahim, 73
  See also Talmud
Pharisee-teachers, 8
Pharisees, 10
  as teachers and judges, 11
  Biblical law, as interpreted by, 145, 146
  Christian criticism of, 153
  Sadducees, differences between this sect and, 24
  Sadducees, replaced by, 24
  scribes, assistance to, by, 24
  Scriptural law, as interpreted by, 145, 146

Talmud and, 11
Philo of Alexandria, 7
Phylacteries (*tephillin*), 74, 75
  See also Tallit
Pontius Pilate, 12
  crucifixion of Jesus, by, 14
Prayer Book, 44, 55
  Psalms, largest source of, 57
  *Siddur,* Hebrew word for, 59
Presbyterians, 134
*Presbyteroi,* 6
*Presbyteros,* 18
Priests, 3, 4, 19
  Judaism, attitude toward, 24
  Scribes, as institution opposed to, 23
Prophets, Books of the 8, 40, 53, 72, 128
  major, 55
  minor (twelve), 55
  writings of, 4
Protestant Bible (King James Version), 53
Protestant clerical stole, 51
Protestantism, "heir" of the synagogue, 33
Protestants, Orthodox, doctrine of, 153
Proverbs, 56
Psalms
  Anglican "Book of Common Prayer," influenced by, 58
  Episcopal "Book of Common Prayer," influenced by, 58
  Hebrew prayers from the, 44, 55, 57, 145
  Protestant churches influenced by, 58
  Roman Catholic Missal, influenced by, 58
  Rosary, based upon, 58
Psalter, Hebrew, 57, 58
Puberty, 71–77
*Purim,* 54

## R

Rabban Gamaliel II, 90
Rabbi, 6, 11
  actual and religious functions of, 26

## Index

Talmud, 11, 60, 61, 62, 73
  Conservatives' acknowledgement
    of authority of, 28
  Rabbis of the, 17, 25, 146
  *See also Gemara; Halakah; Tal-
    mud*
Tammuz, 108
  Seventeenth of, 128
  *See also* Calendar; Temple
*TaNak*, 55
Temple, as contrasted with Syna-
    gogue, 3, 4, 5, 6, 18, 20
  *First*, dedication of, 118
    destruction of, 5, 128
    under Herod, 3
  government of the, 19
  music in the, 47
  religious dress in the, 48, 49
  *Second*, prayer book and, 57
    under Persian rule, 3
  *See also* Hanukkah
Ten Commandments, 71, 99, 126
"Ten Days of Penitence," 109, 112
*Tephillin*, 74, 75, 117
  *See also Tallit*
*Tevet*, 108
  *See also* Calendar
Thirty-nine Books of Old Testa-
    ment, 53, 55
*Tishri*, 108
  *See also* Calendar
Titus, 5
Torah, 7, 8, 36, 39, 40, 41, 44, 61,
    71, 126, 127, 139
  *Bar Mitzvah* and, 72
  component books of, 55
  Messianic tradition and the, 12
  *parochet*, covering the, 36
  Pharisees and the, 10, 11, 24
  precepts of the, 135
  *Simhat Torah* and, 118
  Synagogue reader and the, 35
Torah Ark, 36, 117
Twelve Minor Prophets, 55
Twelve Tribes of Israel, 12

*Tzitzit*, 51
  *See also Tallit*

### U

Universalism, 149, 150
  Christian, 153

### V

*Viddui*, 90
Vulgate, 54
  *See also* Bible

### W

Wesleyanism, 134
Westminster Confession, 134
Women's part in religious life, 75–
    76, 84, 85, 89, 110

### X

### Y

*Yahrzeit*, 59, 92
*Yahweh*, 146
YHVH, 146, 147
*Yetzer ha-ra*, 141
*Yetzer ha-tov*, 141
*Yizkor*, 92
*Yod*, 75
  *See also* Tephillin
*Yom Kippur*, 111, 112, 114
  *See also* Day of Atonement

### Z

Zadok, 10
Zechariah, 55
Zephaniah, 55
Zion, 148
Zion, Mount, 3, 4
*Zucchetto*, 50
  *See also* Dress, religious
Zwinglianism, 134

Index to The New Ecumenism